This book may be ke

WHEELS AND BUTTERFLIES

THE MACMILLAN COMPANY
NEW YORK · BOSTON · CHICAGO · DALLAS
ATLANTA · SAN FRANCISCO

MACMILLAN & CO., Limited
LONDON · BOMBAY · CALCUTTA
MELBOURNE

THE MACMILLAN COMPANY
OF CANADA, Limited
TORONTO

WHEELS
AND
BUTTERFLIES

BY
W. B. YEATS

NEW YORK
THE MACMILLAN COMPANY
1935

Application for the right of performing
these plays or of reading them in public
should be made to Messrs. Samuel
French, 25 West 45th St., New York City.

PRINTED IN THE UNITED STATES OF AMERICA
BY THE STRATFORD PRESS, INC., NEW YORK

To Garret or Cellar a wheel I send,
But every butterfly to a friend.

PREFACE

ALL these plays have been played at the Abbey Theatre, Dublin. *The Words upon the Window-pane* has been revived several times, *The Cat and the Moon* once, but *Fighting the Waves,* which drew large audiences, not at all, because Mr. George Antheil's most strange, most dramatic music requires a large expensive orchestra. A memory of that orchestra has indeed roused a distinguished Irish lyric poet to begin a dance play which he assures me requires but a tin whistle and a large expensive concertina. *The Resurrection* was played for the first time at the Abbey a few days ago. Like *The Cat and the Moon* it was not intended for the public theatre. I permitted it there after great hesitation. Owing perhaps to a strike which has prevented the publication of the religious as well as of the political newspapers and reviews, all is well.

W. B. Y,

4th August 1934

LIST OF CONTENTS

THE WORDS UPON THE WINDOW-PANE

First performed at the Abbey Theatre
on 17th November 1930

IN MEMORY OF

LADY GREGORY

in whose house it was written

PERSONS IN THE PLAY

Dr. Trench
Miss Mackenna
John Corbet
Cornelius Patterson
Abraham Johnson
Mrs. Mallet
Mrs. Henderson

THE WORDS UPON THE WINDOW-PANE

INTRODUCTION

I

SOMEBODY said the other night that Dublin was full of clubs—he himself knew four—that met in cellars and garrets and had for their object our general improvement. He was scornful, said that they had all begun by drawing up a programme and passing a resolution against the censorship and would never do anything else. When I began my public life Dublin was full of such clubs that passed resolutions and drew up programmes, and though the majority did nothing else some helped to find an audience for a school of writers. The fall of Parnell had freed imagination from practical politics, from agrarian grievance and political enmity, and turned it to imaginative nationalism, to Gaelic, to the ancient stories, and at last to lyrical poetry and to drama. Political failure and political success have had the same result except that to-day imagination is turning full of uncertainty to something it thinks European, and whether that something will be 'arty' and provincial, or a form of life, is as yet undiscoverable. Hitherto we have walked the road, but now we have shut the

5

door and turned up the lamp. What shall occupy our imagination? We must, I think, decide among these three ideas of national life: that of Swift; that of a great Italian of his day; that of modern England. If the Garrets and the Cellars listen I may throw light upon the matter, and I hope if all the time I seem thinking of something else I shall be forgiven. I must speak of things that come out of the common consciousness, where every thought is like a bell with many echoes.

My little play *The Words upon the Window-pane* came to me amidst considerations such as these, as a reward, as a moment of excitement. John O'Leary read, during an illness, the poems of Thomas Davis, and though he never thought them good poetry they shaped his future life, gave him the moral simplicity that made him so attractive to young men in his old age, but we can no longer permit life to be shaped by a personified ideal, we must serve with all our faculties some actual thing. The old service was moral, at times lyrical; we discussed perpetually the character of public men and never asked were they able and well-informed, but what would they sacrifice? How many times did I hear on the lips of J. F. Taylor these words: 'Holy, delicate white hands'? His patriotism was a religion, never a philosophy. More extreme in such things than Taylor and O'Leary, who often seemed to live in the eighteenth century, to acknowledge its canons alone in literature and in the arts, I turned from Goldsmith and from

Burke because they had come to seem a part of the English system, from Swift because I acknowledged, being a romantic, no verse between Cowley and Smart's *Song to David,* no prose between Sir Thomas Browne and the *Conversations* of Landor. But now I read Swift for months together, Burke and Berkeley less often but always with excitement, and Goldsmith lures and waits. I collect materials for my thought and work, for some identification of my beliefs with the nation itself, I seek an image of the modern mind's discovery of itself, of its own permanent form, in that one Irish century that escaped from darkness and confusion. I would that our fifteenth, sixteenth, or even our seventeenth century had been the clear mirror, but fate decided against us.

Swift haunts me; he is always just round the next corner. Sometimes it is a thought of my great-great-grandmother, a friend of that Archbishop King who sent him to England about the 'First Fruits,' sometimes it is S. Patrick's, where I have gone to wander and meditate, that brings him to mind, sometimes I remember something hard or harsh in O'Leary or in Taylor, or in the public speech of our statesmen, that reminds me by its style of his verse or prose. Did he not speak, perhaps, with just such an intonation? This instinct for what is near and yet hidden is in reality a return to the sources of our power, and therefore a claim made upon the future. Thought seems more true, emotion more deep, spoken by someone who touches my pride, who seems to claim me of his kindred, who seems to make me a part of some national mythology, nor is mythology mere ostentation, mere vanity if it draws me onward to the unknown; another turn of the gyre and myth is wisdom, pride, discipline. I remember the shudder in my spine when Mrs. Patrick Campbell said, speaking words Hofmannsthal put into the mouth of Electra, 'I too am of that ancient race':

> Swift has sailed into his rest:
> Savage indignation there
> Cannot lacerate his breast.
> Imitate him if you dare,
> World-besotted traveller; he
> Served human liberty.

'In Swift's day men of intellect reached the height of their power, the greatest position they ever attained in society and the State. . . . His ideal order was the Roman Senate, his ideal men Brutus and Cato; such an order and such men had seemed possible once more.' The Cambridge undergraduate into whose mouth I have put these words may have read similar words in Oliver, 'the last brilliant addition to English historians,' for young men such as he read the newest authorities; probably Oliver and he thought of the influence at Court and in public life of Swift and of Leibniz, of the spread of science and of scholarship over Europe, its examination of documents, its destruction of fables, a science and a scholarship modern for the first time, of certain great minds that were medieval in their scope but modern in their freedom. I must, however, add certain thoughts of my own that affected me as I wrote. I thought about a passage in the Grammont *Memoirs* where some great man is commended for his noble manner, as we commend a woman for her beauty or her charm; a famous passage in the *Appeal from the New to the Old Whigs* commending the old Whig aristocracy for their intellect and power and because their doors stood open to like-minded men; the palace of Blenheim, its pride of domination that expected a thousand years, something Asiatic in its carved intricacy of stone.

'Everything great in Ireland and in our character, in what remains of our architecture, comes from that day . . . we have kept its seal longer than England.' The overstatement of an enthusiastic Cambridge student, and yet with its measure of truth. The battle of the Boyne overwhelmed a civilisation full of religion and myth, and brought in its place intelligible laws planned out upon a great blackboard, a capacity for horizontal lines, for rigid shapes, for buildings, for attitudes of mind that could be multiplied like an expanding bookcase: the modern world, and something that appeared and perished in its dawn, an instinct for Roman rhetoric, Roman elegance. It established a Protestant aristocracy, some of whom neither called themselves English [1] nor

---

[1] Nor were they English: the newest arrivals soon intermarried with an older stock, and that older stock had inter-

looked with contempt or dread upon conquered Ireland. Indeed the battle was scarcely over when Molyneux, speaking in their name, affirmed the sovereignty of the Irish Parliament.[1] No one had the right to make our laws but the King, Lords and Commons of Ireland; the battle had been fought to change not an English but an Irish Crown; and our Parliament was almost as ancient as that of England. It was this doctrine [2] that Swift uttered in the fourth *Drapier Letter* with such astringent eloquence that it

married again and again with Gaelic Ireland. All my childhood the Coopers of Markree, County Sligo, represented such rank and fashion as the County knew, and I had it from my friend the late Bryan Cooper that his supposed Cromwellian ancestor being childless adopted an O'Brien; while local tradition thinks that an O'Brien, promised the return of her confiscated estate if she married a Cromwellian soldier, married a Cooper and murdered him three days after. Not, however, before he had founded a family. The family of Yeats, never more than small gentry, arrived, if I can trust the only man among us who may have seen the family tree before it was burnt by Canadian Indians, 'about the time of Henry VII.' Ireland, divided in religion and politics, is as much one race as any modern country.

[1] 'Until 1691 Roman Catholics were admitted by law into both Houses of Legislature in Ireland' (MacNeill's *Constitutional and Parliamentary History of Ireland,* p. 10).

[2] A few weeks ago the hierarchy of the Irish Church addressed, without any mandate from Protestant Ireland, not the Irish people as they had every right to, even in the defence of folly, but the Imperial Conference, and begged that the Irish Courts might remain subservient to the Privy Council. Terrified into intrigue where none threatened, they turned from Swift and Molyneux. I remind them that when the barons of the Irish Court of Exchequer obeyed the English Privy Council in 1719 our ancestors clapped them into gaol. (1931.)

passed from the talk of study and parlour to that of road and market, and created the political nationality of Ireland. Swift found his nationality through the *Drapier Letters,* his convictions came from action and passion, but Berkeley, a much younger man, could find it through contemplation. He and his fellow-students but knew the war through the talk of the older men. As a boy of eighteen or nineteen he called the Irish people 'natives' as though he were in some foreign land, but two or three years later, perhaps while still an undergraduate, defined the English materialism of his day in three profound sentences, and wrote after each that 'we Irishmen' think otherwise—'I publish . . . to know whether other men have the same ideas as we Irishmen'—and before he was twenty-five had fought the Salamis of the Irish intellect. The Irish landed aristocracy, who knew more of the siege of Derry and the battle of the Boyne delineated on vast tapestries for their House of Lords by Dublin Huguenots than of philosophy, found themselves masters of a country demoralised by generations of war and famine and shared in its demoralisation. In 1730 Swift said from the pulpit that their houses were in ruins and no new building anywhere, that the houses of their rack-ridden tenants were no better than English pigsties, that the bulk of the people trod barefoot and in rags. He exaggerated, for already the Speaker, Connolly, had built that great house at Celbridge where slate, stone and furniture were Irish, even the silver from Irish mines; the new Parliament House had perhaps been planned; and there was a general stir of life. The old age of Berkeley passed amid art and music, and men had begun to boast that in these no country had made such progress; and some dozen years after Berkeley's death Arthur Young found everywhere in stately Georgian houses scientific agriculturalists, benefactors of their countryside, though for the half-educated, drunken, fire-eating, impoverished lesser men he had nothing but detestation. Goldsmith might have found likeable qualities, a capacity for mimicry [1] perhaps, among these lesser men, and Sir Jonah Barrington made them his theme, but, detestable or not, they were out of fashion. Miss Edgeworth described her *Castle Rackrent* upon the title-page of its first edition as 'the habits of the Irish squirearchy before 1782.' A few years more and the country people would have forgotten that the Irish aristocracy was founded like all aristocracies upon conquest, or rather, would have remembered, and boasted in the words of a medieval Gaelic poet, 'We are a sword people and we go with the sword.' Unhappily the lesson first taught by Molyneux and Swift had been but half learnt when the test came—country gentlemen are poor politicians—and Ireland's 'dark insipid period' began. During the entire eighteenth century the greatest land-owning family of the neighbourhood I best knew in childhood sent not a single man

[1] He wrote that he had never laughed so much at Garrick's acting as at somebody in an Irish tavern mimicking a Quaker sermon.

into the English army and navy, but during the nineteenth century one or more in every generation; a new absenteeism, foreseen by Miss Edgeworth, began; those that lived upon their estates bought no more fine editions of the classics; separated from public life and ambition they sank, as I have heard Lecky complain, 'into grass farmers.' Yet their genius did not die out; they sent everywhere administrators and military leaders, and now that their ruin has come—what resolute nation permits a strong alien class within its borders?—I would, remembering obscure ancestors that preached in their churches or fought beside their younger sons over half the world, and despite a famous passage of O'Grady's, gladly sing their song.

'He foresaw the ruin to come, Democracy, Rousseau, the French Revolution; that is why he hated the common run of men,—"I hate lawyers, I hate doctors," he said, "though I love Dr. So-and-so and Judge So-and-so,"—that is why he wrote *Gulliver,* that is why he wore out his brain, that is why he felt *saeva indignatio,* that is why he sleeps under the greatest epitaph in history.' The *Discourse of the Contests and Dissensions between the Nobles and the Commons in Athens and Rome,* published in 1703 to warn the Tory Opposition of the day against the impeachment of Ministers, is Swift's one philosophical work. All States depend for their health upon a right balance between the One, the Few, and the Many. The One is the executive, which may in fact be more than one—the Roman republic had two Consuls—but must for the sake of rapid decision be as few as possible; the Few are those who through the possession of hereditary wealth, or great personal gifts, have come to identify their lives with the life of the State, whereas the lives and ambitions of the Many are private. The Many do their day's work well, and so far from copying even the wisest of their neighbours affect 'a singularity' in action and in thought; but set them to the work of the State and every man Jack is 'listed in a party,' becomes the fanatical follower of men of whose characters he knows next to nothing, and from that day on puts nothing into his mouth some other man has not already chewed and digested. And furthermore, from the moment of enlistment thinks himself above other men and struggles for power until all is in confusion. I divine an Irish hatred of abstraction likewise expressed by that fable of Gulliver among the inventors and men of science, by Berkeley in his *Commonplace Book,* by Goldsmith in the satire of *The Good-Natured Man,* in the picturesque, minute observation of *The Deserted Village,* and by Burke in his attack upon mathematical democracy. Swift enforced his moral by proving that Rome and Greece were destroyed by the war of the Many upon the Few; in Rome, where the Few had kept their class organisation, it was a war of classes, in Greece, where they had not, war upon character and genius. Miltiades, Aristides, Themistocles, Pericles, Alcibiades, Phocion, 'impeached for high crimes and misdemeanours . . . were honoured and lamented by their country as the preservers of it, and have had the veneration of all ages since paid justly to their memories.' In Rome parties so developed that men born and bred among the Few were compelled to join one party or the other and to flatter and bribe. All civilisations must end in some such way, for the Many obsessed by emotion create a multitude of religious sects but give themselves at last to some one master of bribes and flatteries and sink into the ignoble tranquillity of servitude. He defines a tyranny as the predominance of the One, the Few, or the Many, but thinks that of the Many the immediate threat. All States at their outset possess a ruling power seated in the whole body as that of the soul in the human body, a perfect balance of the three estates, the king some sort of chief magistrate, and then comes 'a tyranny: first either of the Few or the Many; but at last infallibly of a single person.' He thinks the English balance most perfect in the time of Queen Elizabeth, but that in the next age a tyranny of the Many produced that of Cromwell, and that, though recovery followed, 'all forms of government must be mortal like their authors,' and he quotes from Polybius, 'those abuses and corruptions, which in time destroy a government, are sown along with the very seeds of it' and destroy it 'as rust eats away iron, and worms devour wood.' Whether the final tyranny is created by the Many—in his eyes all Caesars were tyrants—or imposed by foreign power, the result is the same.

At the fall of liberty came 'a dark insipid period through all Greece'—had he Ireland in his mind also?—and the people became, in the words of Polybius, 'great reverencers of crowned heads.'

Twenty-two years later Giambattista Vico published that *Scienza Nuova* which Mr. James Joyce is expounding or symbolising in the strange fragments of his *Work in Progress*. He was the opposite of Swift in everything, an humble, peaceful man, son of a Neapolitan bookseller and without political opinions; he wrote panegyrics upon men of rank, seemed to admire all that they did, took their gratuities and yet kept his dignity. He thought civilisation passed through the phases Swift has described, but that it was harsh and terrible until the Many prevailed, and its joints cracked and loosened, happiest when some one man, surrounded by able subordinates, dismissed the Many to their private business, that its happiness lasted some generations until, sense of the common welfare lost, it grew malicious and treacherous, fell into 'the barbarism of reflection,' and after that into an honest, plain barbarism accepted with relief by all and started upon its round again. Rome had conquered surrounding nations because those nations were nearer than it to humanity and happiness; was not Carthage already almost a democratic state when destruction came? Swift seemed to shape his narrative upon some clairvoyant vision of his own life, for he saw civilisation pass from comparative happiness and youthful vigour to an old age of violence and self-contempt, whereas Vico saw it begin in penury like himself and end as he himself would end in a long inactive peace. But there was a greater difference; Swift, a practical politician in everything he wrote, ascribed its rise and fall to virtues and vices all could understand, whereas the philosophical Vico ascribed them to 'the rhythm of the elemental forms of the mind,' a new idea that would dominate philosophy. Outside Anglo-Saxon nations where progress, impelled by moral enthusiasm and the Patent Office, seems a perpetual straight line, this 'circular movement,' as Swift's master, Polybius, called it, has long been the friend and enemy of public order. Both Sorel and Marx, their eyes more Swift's than Vico's, have preached a return to a primeval state, a beating of all down into a single class that a new civilisation may arise with its Few, its Many, and its One. Students of contemporary Italy, where Vico's thought is current through its influence upon Croce and Gentile, think it created, or in part created, the present government of one man surrounded by just such able assistants as Vico foresaw. Some philosopher has added this further thought: the classes rise out of the matrix, create all mental and bodily riches, sink back, as Vico saw civilisation rise and sink, and government is there to keep the ring and see to it that combat never ends. These thoughts in the next few generations, as elaborated by Oswald Spengler, who has followed Vico without essential change, by Flinders Petrie, by the German traveller Frobenius, by Henry Adams, and perhaps by my friend Gerald Heard, may affect the masses. They have already deepened our sense of tragedy and somewhat checked the naïver among those creeds and parties who push their way to power by flattering our moral hopes. Pascal thought there was evidence for and against the existence of God, but that if a man kept his mind in suspense about it he could not live a rich and active life, and I suggest to the Cellars and Garrets that though history is too short to change either the idea of progress or the eternal circuit into scientific fact, the eternal circuit may best suit our preoccupation with the soul's salvation, our individualism, our solitude. Besides we love antiquity, and that other idea—progress—the sole religious myth of modern man, is only two hundred years old.

Swift's pamphlet had little effect in its day; it did not prevent the impeachment and banishment a few years later of his own friends; and although he was in all probability the first—if there was another 'my small reading cannot trace it'—to describe in terms of modern politics the discord of parties that compelled revolutionary France, as it has compelled half a dozen nations since the war, to accept the 'tyranny' of a 'single person,' it was soon forgotten; but for the understanding of Swift it is essential. It shows that the defence of liberty boasted upon his tombstone did not come from political disappointment (when he wrote it he had suffered none); and what he meant by liberty. Gulliver, in those travels written twenty years later, calls up from the dead 'a sex-tumvirate to which all the ages of the world cannot add a seventh': Epaminondas and Socrates, who suffered at the hands of the Many; Brutus, Junius Brutus, Cato the Younger, Thomas More, who fought the tyranny of the One; Brutus with Caesar still his inseparable friend, for a man may be a tyrant without personal guilt.

Liberty depended upon a balance within the State, like that of the 'humours' in a human body, or like that 'unity of being' Dante compared to a perfectly proportioned human body, and for its sake Swift was prepared to sacrifice what seems to the modern man liberty itself. The odds were a hundred to one, he wrote, that 'violent zeal for the truth' came out of 'petulancy, ambition, or pride.' He himself might prefer a republic to a monarchy, but did he open his mouth upon the subject would be deservedly hanged. Had he religious doubts he was not to blame so long as he kept them to himself, for God had given him reason. It was the attitude of many a modern Catholic who thinks, though upon different grounds, that our civilisation may sink into a decadence like that of Rome. But sometimes belief itself must be hidden. He was devout; had the Communion Service by heart; read the Fathers and prayed much, yet would not press the mysteries of his faith upon any unwilling man. Had not the early Christians kept silent about the divinity of Christ; should not the missionaries to China 'soften' it? He preached as law com-

manded; a man could save his soul doubtless in any
religion which taught submission to the Will of God,
but only one State could protect his body; and how
could it protect his body if rent apart by those cranks
and sectaries mocked in his *Tale of a Tub?* Had not
French Huguenots and English Dissenters alike
sinned against the State? Except at those moments of
great public disturbance, when a man must choose
his creed or his king, let him think his own thoughts
in silence.

What was this liberty bought with so much silence,
and served through all his life with so much eloquence? 'I should think,' he wrote in the *Discourse,*
'that the saying, *vox populi, vox dei* ought to be understood of the universal bent and current of a people, not of the bare majority of a few representatives,
which is often procured by little arts, and great in-
dustry and application; wherein those who engage in
the pursuits of malice and revenge are much more
sedulous than such as would prevent them.' That *vox
populi* or 'bent and current,' or what we even more
vaguely call national spirit, was the sole theme of his
Drapier Letters; its right to express itself as it would
through such men as had won or inherited general
consent. I doubt if a mind so contemptuous of average men thought, as Vico did, that it found expression also through all individual lives, or asked more
for those lives than protection from the most obvious
evils. I remember J. F. Taylor, a great student of

Swift, saying 'individual liberty is of no importance, what matters is national liberty.'

The will of the State, whether it build a cage for a dead bird or remain in the bird itself, must always, whether interpreted by Burke or Marx, find expression through some governing class or company identified with that 'bent and current,' with those 'elemental forms,' whether by interest or training. The men of Swift's day would have added that class or company must be placed by wealth above fear and toil, though Swift thought every properly conducted State must limit the amount of wealth the individual could possess. But the old saying that there is no wisdom without leisure has somewhat lost its truth. When the physical world became rigid; when curiosity inherited from the Renaissance, and the soul's anxiety inherited from the Middle Ages, passed, man ceased to think; his work thought in him. Spinoza, Leibniz, Swift, Berkeley, Goethe, the last typical figure of the epoch, recognised no compulsion but the 'bent and current' of their lives; the Speaker, Connolly, could still call out a posse of gentlemen to design the façade of his house, and though Berkeley thought their number too great, that work is still admired; Swift called himself a poor scholar in comparison with Lord Treasurer Harley. Unity of being was still possible though somewhat over-rationalised and abstract, more diagram than body; whereas the best modern philosophers are professors, their pupils compile notebooks that they may be professors some day; politicians stick to their last or leave it to plague us with platitudes; we poets and artists may be called, so small our share in life, 'separated spirits,' words applied by the old philosophers to the dead. When Swift sank into imbecility or madness his epoch had finished in the British Isles, those 'elemental forms' had passed beyond him; more than the 'great Ministers' had gone. I can see in a sort of nightmare vision the 'primary qualities' torn from the side of Locke, Johnson's ponderous body bent above the letter to Lord Chesterfield, some obscure person somewhere inventing the spinning-jenny, upon his face that look of benevolence kept by painters and engravers, from the middle of the eighteenth century to the time of the Prince Consort, for such as he, or, to simplify the tale—

> Locke sank into a swoon;
> The Garden died;
> God took the spinning-jenny
> Out of his side.

'That arrogant intellect free at last from superstition': the young man's overstatement full of the unexamined suppositions of common speech. I saw Asia in the carved stones of Blenheim, not in the pride of great abstract masses, but in that humility of flowerlike intricacy—the particular blades of the grass; nor can chance have thrown into contiguous generations Spinoza and Swift, an absorption of the whole intellect in God, a fakir-like contempt for all human desire; 'take from her,' Swift prayed for Stella in sickness, 'all violent desire whether of life or death'; the elaboration and spread of Masonic symbolism, its God made in the image of a Christopher Wren; Berkeley's declaration, modified later, that physical pleasure is the *Summum Bonum,* Heaven's sole reality, his counter-truth to that of Spinoza.

In judging any moment of past time we should leave out what has since happened; we should not call the Swift of the *Drapier Letters* nearer truth because of their influence upon history than the Swift who attacked in *Gulliver* the inventors and logicians; we should see certain men and women as if at the edge of a cliff, time broken away from their feet. Spinoza and the Masons, Berkeley and Swift, speculative and practical intellect, stood there free at last from all prepossessions and touched the extremes of thought; the Gymnosophists of Strabo close at hand, could they but ignore what was harsh and logical in themselves, or the China of the Dutch cabinet-makers, of the *Citizen of the World:* the long-settled rule of powerful men, no great dogmatic structure, few great crowded streets, scattered unprogressive communities, much handiwork, wisdom wound into the roots of the grass.

'I have something in my blood that no child must inherit.' There have been several theories to account for Swift's celibacy. Sir Walter Scott suggested a 'physical defect,' but that seems incredible. A man so outspoken would have told Vanessa the truth and stopped a tragic persecution, a man so charitable have given Stella the protection of his name. The refusal to see Stella when there was no third person present suggests a man that dreaded temptation; nor is it compatible with those stories still current among our country people of Swift sending his servant out to fetch a woman, and dismissing that servant when he woke to find a black woman at his side. Lecky suggested dread of madness—the theory of my play— of madness already present in constant eccentricity; though, with a vagueness born from distaste of the theme, he saw nothing incompatible between Scott's theory and his own. Had Swift dreaded transmitting madness he might well have been driven to consorting with the nameless barren women of the streets. Somebody else suggests syphilis contracted doubtless between 1799 when he was engaged to Varina and some date soon after Stella's arrival in Ireland. Mr. Shane Leslie thinks that Swift's relation to Vanessa was not platonic,[1] and that whenever his letters speak of a cup of coffee they mean the sexual act; whether the letters seem to bear him out I do not know, for those letters bore me; but whether they seem to or not he must, if he is to get a hearing, account for Swift's relation to Stella. It seems certain that Swift loved her though he called it by some other name, and she him, and that it was platonic love.

[1] Rossi and Hone take the same view, though uncertain about the coffee. When I wrote, their book had not appeared.

Thou, Stella, wert no longer young,
When first for thee my harp was strung,
Without one word of Cupid's darts,
Of killing eyes or bleeding hearts;
With friendship and esteem possest,
I ne'er admitted Love a guest.
In all the habitudes of life,
The friend, the mistress, and the wife,
Variety we still pursue,
In pleasure seek for something new;
Or else comparing with the rest,
Take comfort that our own is best;
The best we value by the worst,
As tradesmen show their trash at first;
But his pursuits are at an end,
Whom Stella chooses for a friend.

If the relation between Swift and Vanessa was not platonic there must have been some bar that affected Stella as well as Swift. Dr. Delaney is said to have believed that Swift married Stella in 1716 and found in some exchange of confidences that they were brother and sister, but Sir William Temple was not in Ireland during the year that preceded Swift's birth, and so far as we know Swift's mother was not in England.

There is no satisfactory solution. Swift, though he lived in great publicity, and wrote and received many letters, hid two things which constituted perhaps all that he had of private life: his loves and his religious beliefs.

'Was Swift mad? Or was it the intellect itself that was mad?' The other day a scholar in whose imagination Swift has a pre-eminence scarcely possible outside Ireland said: 'I sometimes feel that there is a black cloud about to overwhelm me, and then comes a great jet of life; Swift had that black cloud and no jet. He was terrified.' I said, 'Terrified perhaps of everything but death,' and reminded him of a story of Dr. Johnson's.[1] There was a reward of £500 for the identification of the author of the *Drapier Letters*. Swift's butler, who had carried the manuscript to the printer, stayed away from work. When he returned Swift said, 'I know that my life is in your hands, but I will not bear, out of fear, either your insolence or negligence.' He dismissed the butler, and when the danger had passed he restored him to his post, rewarded him, and said to the other servants, 'No more Barclay, henceforth Mr. Barclay.' 'Yes,' said my friend, 'he was not afraid of death but of life, of what might happen next; that is what made him so defiant in public and in private and demand for the State the obedience a Connacht priest demands for the Church.' I have put a cognate thought into the mind of John Corbet. He imagines, though but for a moment, that the intellect of Swift's age, persuaded that the mechanicians mocked by Gulliver would prevail, that its moment of freedom could not last, so dreaded the historic process that it became in the half-mad mind of Swift a dread of parentage:

[1] Sheridan has a different version, but as I have used it merely to illustrate an argument I leave it as Dr. Johnson told it.

'Am I to add another to the healthy rascaldom and knavery of the world?' Did not Rousseau within five years of the death of Swift publish his *Discourse upon Arts and Sciences* and discover instinctive harmony not in heroic effort, not in Cato and Brutus, not among impossible animals—I think of that noble horse Blake drew for Hayley—but among savages, and thereby beget the sans-culottes of Marat? After the arrogance of power the humility of a servant.

II

When I went into the theatre café after the performance a woman asked a question and I replied with some spiritualistic anecdote. 'Did that happen with the medium we have seen to-night?' she said: and yet May Craig who played the part had never seen a séance. I had, however, assisted her by self-denial. No character upon the stage spoke my thoughts. All were people I had met or might have met in just such a séance. Taken as a whole, the man who expected to find whippet-racing beyond the grave, not less than the old man who was half a Swedenborgian, expresses an attitude of mind of millions who have substituted the séance-room for the church. At most séances there is somebody who finds symbol where his neighbour finds fact, but the average man or woman thinks that the dead have houses, that they eat and sleep, hear lectures, or occasionally talk with Christ as though He were a living man; and certainly the voices are at times so natural, the forms so solid, that the plain man can scarce think otherwise.

If I had not denied myself, if I had allowed some character to speak my thoughts, what would he have said? It seems to me that after reading many books and meeting many phenomena, some in my own house, some when alone in my room, I can see clearly at last. I consider it certain that every voice that speaks, every form that appears, whether to the medium's eyes and ears alone or to some one or two others or to all present, whether it remains a sight or sound or affects the sense of touch, whether it is confined to the room or can make itself apparent at some distant place, whether it can or cannot alter the position of material objects, is first of all a secondary personality or dramatisation created by, in, or through the medium. Perhaps May Craig, when alone in her room after the play, went, without knowing what she was doing, through some detail of her performance. I once saw an Abbey actor going up the stairs to his dressing-room after playing the part of a lame man and saw that he was still limping. I see no difference except one of degree between such unconscious movements and the strange powerful grotesque faces imprinted by the controls of Eusapia Palladino upon paraffin wax. The Polish psychologist Ochorowicz, vexed by the mischievous character of his medium's habitual control, created by suggestion a docile and patient substitute that left a photograph of its hand and arm upon an unopened coil of film in a sealed bottle. But at most séances the suggestions come from sub-conscious or unspoken thought. I found the preacher who wanted Moody's help at a séance where the mind of an old doting general turned all into delirium. We sat in the dark and voices came about us in the air; crowned head after crowned head spoke until Cromwell intervened and was abused by one of the sitters for cutting off the head of 'Charles the Second,' while the preacher kept repeating, 'He is monopolising the séance, I want Mr. Moody, it is most important I should get Mr. Moody.' Then came a voice, 'King George is here.' I asked which of the Georges, and the sitter who hated Cromwell said, 'King George, our George; we should all stand up,' but the general thought it would be enough if we sang 'God save the King.' We sang, and then there was silence, and in the silence from somewhere close to the ceiling the clear song of a bird. Because mediumship is dramatisation : even honest mediums cheat at times either deliberately or because some part of the body has freed itself from the control of the waking will, and almost always truth and lies are mixed together. But what shall we say of their knowledge of events, their assumption of forms and names beyond the medium's knowledge or ours? What of the arm photographed in the bottle?

The Indian ascetic passing into his death-like trance knows that if his mind is not pure, if there is anything there but the symbol of his God, some passion, ambition, desire, or phantasy will confer upon him its shape or purpose, for he is entering upon a state where thought and existence are the same. One remembers those witches described by Glanvil who course the field in the likeness of hares while their bodies lie at home, and certain mediumistic phenomena. The ascetic would say, did we question him, that the unpurified dead are subject to transformations that would be similar were it not that in their case no physical body remains in cave or bed or chair, all is transformed. They examine their past undisturbed by our importunity, tracing events to their source, and as they take the form their thought suggests, seem to live backward through time; or if incapable of such examination, creatures not of thought but of feeling, renew as shades certain detached events of their past lives, taking the greater excitements first. When Achilles came to the edge of the blood-pool (an ancient substitute for the medium) he was such a shade. Tradition affirms that, deprived of the living present by death, they can create nothing, or, in the Indian phrase, can originate no new Karma. Their aim, like that of the ascetic in meditation, is to enter at last into their own archetype, or into all being: into that which is there always. They are not, however, the personalities which haunt the séance-room: these when they speak from, or imply, supernormal knowledge, when they are more than transformations of the medium, are, as it were, new beings begotten by spirit upon medium to live short but veritable lives, whereas the secondary personalities resemble those eggs brought forth without the assistance of the male bird. They, within their narrow limits, create; they speak truth when they repeat some message suggested by the past lives of the spirit, remembered like some prenatal memory, or when, though such instances must be few, begotten by some spirit obedient to its source, or, as we might say, blessed; but when they neither repeat such message nor were so begotten they may justify passages in Swedenborg that denounce them as the newspapers denounce cheating mediums, seeing that they find but little check in their fragmentary knowledge or vague conscience.

Let images of basalt, black, immovable,
Chiselled in Egypt, or ovoids of bright steel
Hammered and polished by Brancusi's hand,
Represent spirits. If spirits seem to stand
Before the bodily eyes, speak into the bodily ears,
They are not present but their messengers.
Of double nature these, one nature is
Compounded of accidental phantasies.
We question; it but answers what we would
Or as phantasy directs—because they have drunk the
    blood.

I have not heard of spirits in a European séance-room re-enacting their past lives; our séances take their characteristics from the desire of those present to speak to, or perhaps obtain the counsel of, their dead; yet under the conditions described in my play such re-enacting might occur, indeed most hauntings are of that nature. Here, however, is a French travel-ler's account of a séance in Madagascar, quoted by César de Vesme:

. . . One, Taimandebakaka, of the Bara race, and renowned in the valley of the Menamaty as a great sorcerer, evoked one day in my presence in his village the souls of Captain Flayelle and of Lieutenant Mon-tagnole, both killed at Vohingheso in a fight with the Baras four years before. Those present—myself and some privileged natives—saw nothing when Taimande-bakaka claimed to see the two persons in question; but we could hear the voices of officers issuing orders to their soldiers, and these voices were European voices which could not be imitated by natives. Similarly, at a distance we could hear the echoes of firing and the cries of the wounded and the lowing of frightened cattle—oxen of the Fahavalos.

III

It is fitting that Plotinus should have been the first philosopher to meet his daimon face to face, though the boy attendant out of jealousy or in convulsive terror strangled the doves, for he was the first to establish as sole source the timeless individuality or daimon instead of the Platonic Idea, to prefer Socrates to his thought. This timeless individuality contains archetypes of all possible existences whether of man or brute, and as it traverses its circle of al-lotted lives, now one, now another, prevails. We may fail to express an archetype or alter it by reason, but all done from nature is its unfolding into time. Some other existence may take the place of Socrates, yet Socrates can never cease to exist. Once a friend of mine was digging in a long-neglected garden and suddenly out of the air came a voice thanking her, an old owner of the garden, she was told later, long since reborn, yet still in the garden. Plotinus said that we should not 'baulk at this limitlessness of the intellectual; it is an infinitude having nothing to do with number or part' (*Ennead V. 7.* I.) ; yet it seems that it can at will re-enter number and part and thereby make itself apparent to our minds. If we accept this idea many strange or beautiful things become credible. The Indian pilgrim has not deceived us; he did hear the bed where the sage of his devotion slept a thousand years ago creak as though someone turned over in it, and he did see—he himself and the old shrine-keeper—the blankets all tossed about at dawn as if someone had just risen; the Irish country-woman did see the ruined castle lit up, the bridge across the river dropping; those two Oxford ladies did find themselves in the garden of the Petit Trianon with Marie Antoinette and her courtiers, see that garden as those saw it; the gamekeeper did hear those footsteps the other night that sounded like the footsteps of a stag where stag has not passed these hundred years. All about us there seems to start up a precise inexplicable teeming life, and the earth becomes once more, not in rhetorical metaphor, but in reality, sacred.

1931

THE WORDS UPON THE WINDOW-PANE

A lodging-house room, an armchair, a little table in front of it, chairs on either side. A fireplace and window. A kettle on the hob and some tea-things on a dresser. A door to back and towards the right. Through the door one can see an entrance hall. The sound of a knocker. Miss Mackenna passes through and then she re-enters the hall together with John Corbet, a man of twenty-two or twenty-three, and Dr. Trench, a man of between sixty and seventy.

DR. TRENCH [*in hall*]. May I introduce John Corbet, one of the Corbets of Ballymoney, but at present a Cambridge student? This is Miss Mackenna, our energetic secretary. [*They come into room, take off their coats.*]

MISS MACKENNA. I thought it better to let you in myself. This country is still sufficiently medieval to make spiritualism an undesirable theme for gossip. Give me your coats and hats, I will put them in my own room. It is just across the hall. Better sit down; your watches must be fast. Mrs. Henderson is lying down, as she always does before a séance. We won't begin for ten minutes yet. [*She goes out with hats and coats.*]

DR. TRENCH. Miss Mackenna does all the real work of the Dublin Spiritualists' Association. She did all the correspondence with Mrs. Henderson, and persuaded the landlady to let her this big room and a small room upstairs. We are a poor society and could not guarantee anything in advance. Mrs. Henderson has come from London at her own risk. She was born in Dublin and wants to spread the movement here. She lives very economically and does not expect a great deal. We all give what we can. A poor woman with the soul of an apostle.

JOHN CORBET. Have there been many séances?

DR. TRENCH. Only three so far.

JOHN CORBET. I hope she will not mind my scepticism. I have looked into Myers' *Human Personality* and a wild book by Conan Doyle, but am unconvinced.

DR. TRENCH. We all have to find the truth for ourselves. Lord Dunraven, then Lord Adare, introduced my father to the famous David Home. My father often told me that he saw David Home floating in the air in broad daylight, but I did not believe a word of it. I had to investigate for myself, and I was very hard to convince. Mrs. Piper, an American trance medium, not unlike Mrs. Henderson, convinced me.

JOHN CORBET. A state of somnambulism and voices coming through her lips that purport to be those of dead persons?

DR. TRENCH. Exactly: quite the best kind of mediumship if you want to establish the identity of a spirit. But do not expect too much. There has been a hostile influence.

JOHN CORBET. You mean an evil spirit?

DR. TRENCH. The poet Blake said that he never knew a bad man that had not something very good about him. I say a hostile influence, an influence that disturbed the last séance very seriously. I cannot tell you what happened, for I have not been at any of Mrs. Henderson's séances. Trance mediumship has nothing new to show me—I told the young people when they made me their President that I would probably stay at home, that I could get more out of Emanuel Swedenborg than out of any séance. [*A knock.*] That is probably old Cornelius Patterson; he thinks they race horses and whippets in the other world, and is, so they tell me, so anxious to find out if he is right that he is always punctual. Miss Mackenna will keep him to herself for some minutes. He gives her tips for Harold's Cross.

[*Miss Mackenna crosses to hall door and admits Cornelius Patterson. She brings him to her room across the hall.*

JOHN CORBET [*who has been wandering about*]. This is a wonderful room for a lodging-house.

DR. TRENCH. It was a private house until about fifty years ago. It was not so near the town in those days, and there are large stables at the back. Quite a number of notable people lived here. Grattan was born upstairs; no, not Grattan, Curran perhaps—I forget—but I do know that this house in the early part of the eighteenth century belonged to friends of Jonathan Swift, or rather of Stella. Swift chaffed her in the *Journal to Stella* because of certain small sums of money she lost at cards probably in this very room. That was before Vanessa appeared upon the scene. It was a country-house in those days, surrounded by trees and gardens. Somebody cut some lines from a poem of hers upon the window-pane— tradition says Stella herself. [*A knock.*] Here they are, but you will hardly make them out in this light. [*They stand in the window. Corbet stoops down to see better. Miss Mackenna and Abraham Johnson enter and stand near door.*]

ABRAHAM JOHNSON. Where is Mrs. Henderson?

MISS MACKENNA. She is upstairs; she always rests before a séance.

ABRAHAM JOHNSON. I must see her before the séance. I know exactly what to do to get rid of this evil influence.

MISS MACKENNA. If you go up to see her there will be no séance at all. She says it is dangerous even to think, much less to speak, of an evil influence.

ABRAHAM JOHNSON. Then I shall speak to the President.

MISS MACKENNA. Better talk the whole thing over first in my room. Mrs. Henderson says that there must be perfect harmony.

ABRAHAM JOHNSON. Something must be done. The last séance was completely spoilt. [*A knock.*]

MISS MACKENNA. That may be Mrs. Mallet; she

is a very experienced spiritualist. Come to my room, old Patterson and some others are there already. [*She brings him to the other room and later crosses to hall door to admit Mrs. Mallet.*]

JOHN CORBET. I know those lines well—they are part of a poem Stella wrote for Swift's fifty-fourth birthday. Only three poems of hers—and some lines she added to a poem of Swift's—have come down to us, but they are enough to prove her a better poet than Swift. Even those few words on the window make me think of a seventeenth-century poet, Donne or Crashaw. [*He quotes*]

> 'You taught how I might youth prolong
> By knowing what is right and wrong,
> How from my heart to bring supplies
> Of lustre to my fading eyes.'

How strange that a celibate scholar, well on in life, should keep the love of two such women! He met Vanessa in London at the height of his political power. She followed him to Dublin. She loved him for nine years, perhaps died of love, but Stella loved him all her life.

DR. TRENCH. I have shown that writing to several persons, and you are the first who has recognised the lines.

JOHN CORBET. I am writing an essay on Swift and Stella for my doctorate at Cambridge. I hope to prove that in Swift's day men of intellect reached the height of their power—the greatest position they ever attained in society and the State, that everything great in Ireland and in our character, in what remains of our architecture, comes from that day; that we have kept its seal longer than England.

DR. TRENCH. A tragic life; Bolingbroke, Harley, Ormonde, all those great Ministers that were his friends, banished and broken.

JOHN CORBET. I do not think you can explain him in that way—his tragedy had deeper foundations. His ideal order was the Roman Senate, his ideal men Brutus and Cato. Such an order and such men had seemed possible once more, but the movement passed and he foresaw the ruin to come, Democracy, Rousseau, the French Revolution; that is why he hated the common run of men,—'I hate lawyers, I hate doctors,' he said, 'though I love Dr. So-and-so and Judge So-and-so'—that is why he wrote *Gulliver,* that is why he wore out his brain, that is why he felt *saeva indignatio,* that is why he sleeps under the greatest epitaph in history. You remember how it goes? It is almost finer in English than in Latin: 'He has gone where fierce indignation can lacerate his heart no more.'

[*Abraham Johnson comes in, followed by Mrs. Mallet and Cornelius Patterson.*

ABRAHAM JOHNSON. Something must be done, Dr. Trench, to drive away the influence that has destroyed our séances. I have come here week after week at considerable expense. I am from Belfast. I am by profession a minister of the Gospel, I do a great deal of work among the poor and ignorant. I produce considerable effect by singing and preaching, but I know that my effect should be much greater than it is. My hope is that I shall be able to communicate with the great Evangelist Moody. I want to ask him to stand invisible beside me when I speak or sing, and lay his hands upon my head and give me such a portion of his power that my work may be blessed as the work of Moody and Sankey was blessed.

MRS. MALLET. What Mr. Johnson says about the hostile influence is quite true. The last two séances were completely spoilt. I am thinking of starting a teashop in Folkestone. I followed Mrs. Henderson to Dublin to get my husband's advice, but two spirits kept talking and would not let any other spirit say a word.

DR. TRENCH. Did the spirits say the same thing and go through the same drama at both séances?

MRS. MALLET. Yes—just as if they were characters in some kind of horrible play.

DR. TRENCH. That is what I was afraid of.

MRS. MALLET. My husband was drowned at sea ten years ago, but constantly speaks to me through Mrs. Henderson as if he were still alive. He advises me about everything I do, and I am utterly lost if I cannot question him.

CORNELIUS PATTERSON. I never did like the Heaven they talk about in churches; but when somebody told me that Mrs. Mallet's husband ate and

drank and went about with his favourite dog, I said
to myself, 'That is the place for Corney Patterson.'
I came here to find out if it was true, and I declare
to God I have not heard one word about it.

ABRAHAM JOHNSON. I ask you, Dr. Trench, as
President of the Dublin Spiritualists' Association, to
permit me to read the ritual of exorcism appointed
for such occasions. After the last séance I copied it
out of an old book in the library of Belfast Univer-
sity. I have it here.

[*He takes paper out of his pocket.*

DR. TRENCH. The spirits are people like ourselves,
we treat them as our guests and protect them from
discourtesy and violence, and every exorcism is a
curse or a threatened curse. We do not admit that
there are evil spirits. Some spirits are earth-bound—
they think they are still living and go over and over
some action of their past lives, just as we go over
and over some painful thought, except that where
they are thought is reality. For instance, when a spirit
which has died a violent death comes to a medium
for the first time, it relives all the pains of death.

MRS. MALLET. When my husband came for the
first time the medium gasped and struggled as if she
was drowning. It was terrible to watch.

DR. TRENCH. Sometimes a spirit re-lives not the
pain of death but some passionate or tragic moment
of life. Swedenborg describes this and gives the reason for it. There is an incident of the kind in the
Odyssey, and many in Eastern literature; the mur-

derer repeats his murder, the robber his robbery, the lover his serenade, the soldier hears the trumpet once again. If I were a Catholic I would say that such spirits were in Purgatory. In vain do we write *requiescat in pace* upon the tomb, for they must suffer, and we in our turn must suffer until God gives peace. Such spirits do not often come to séances unless those séances are held in houses where those spirits lived, or where the event took place. This spirit which speaks those incomprehensible words and does not answer when spoken to is of such a nature. The more patient we are, the more quickly will it pass out of its passion and its remorse.

ABRAHAM JOHNSON. I am still convinced that the spirit which disturbed the last séance is evil. If I may not exorcise it I will certainly pray for protection.

DR. TRENCH. Mrs. Henderson's control, Lulu, is able and experienced and can protect both medium and sitters, but it may help Lulu if you pray that the spirit find rest.

> [*Abraham Johnson sits down and prays silently, moving his lips. Mrs. Henderson comes in with Miss Mackenna and others. Miss Mackenna shuts the door.*

DR. TRENCH. Mrs. Henderson, may I introduce to you Mr. Corbet, a young man from Cambridge and a sceptic, who hopes that you will be able to convince him?

MRS. HENDERSON. We were all sceptics once. He must not expect too much from a first séance. He must persevere. [*She sits in the armchair, and the others begin to seat themselves. Miss Mackenna goes to John Corbet and they remain standing.*]

MISS MACKENNA. I am glad that you are a sceptic.

JOHN CORBET. I thought you were a spiritualist.

MISS MACKENNA. I have seen a good many séances, and sometimes think it is all coincidence and thought-transference. [*She says this in a low voice.*] Then at other times I think as Dr. Trench does, and then I feel like Job—you know the quotation—the hair of my head stands up. A spirit passes before my face.

MRS. MALLET. Turn the key, Dr. Trench, we don't want anybody blundering in here. [*Dr. Trench locks door.*] Come and sit here, Miss Mackenna.

MISS MACKENNA. No, I am going to sit beside Mr. Corbet.   [*Corbet and Miss Mackenna sit down.*

JOHN CORBET. You feel like Job to-night?

MISS MACKENNA. I feel that something is going to happen, that is why I am glad that you are a sceptic.

JOHN CORBET. You feel safer?

MISS MACKENNA. Yes, safer.

MRS. HENDERSON. I am glad to meet all my dear friends again and to welcome Mr. Corbet amongst us. As he is a stranger I must explain that we do not call up spirits: we make the right conditions and they come. I do not know who is going to come; sometimes there are a great many and the guides choose between them. The guides try to send somebody for everybody but do not always succeed. If you want to speak to some dear friend who has passed over, do not be discouraged. If your friend cannot come this time, maybe he can next time. My control is a dear little girl called Lulu who died when she was five or six years old. She describes the spirits present and tells us what spirit wants to speak. Miss Mackenna, a verse of a hymn, please, the same we had last time, and will everyone join in the singing?

> [*They sing the following lines from Hymn 564, Dublin Church Hymnal.*

'Sun of my soul, Thou Saviour dear,
It is not night if Thou be near:
O may no earth-born cloud arise
To hide Thee from Thy servant's eyes.'

> [*Mrs. Henderson is leaning back in her chair asleep.*

MISS MACKENNA [*to John Corbet*]. She always snores like that when she is going off.

MRS. HENDERSON [*in a child's voice*]. Lulu so glad to see all her friends.

MRS. MALLET. And we are glad you have come, Lulu.

MRS. HENDERSON [*in a child's voice*]. Lulu glad to see new friend.

MISS MACKENNA [*to John Corbet*]. She is speaking to you.

JOHN CORBET. Thank you, Lulu.

MRS. HENDERSON [*in a child's voice*]. You mustn't laugh at the way I talk.

JOHN CORBET. I am not laughing, Lulu.

MRS. HENDERSON [*in a child's voice*]. Nobody must laugh. Lulu does her best but can't say big long words. Lulu sees a tall man here, lots of hair on face [*Mrs. Henderson passes her hands over her cheeks and chin*], not much on the top of his head [*Mrs. Henderson passes her hand over the top of her head*], red necktie, and such a funny sort of pin.

MRS. MALLET. Yes. . . . Yes. . . .

MRS. HENDERSON [*in a child's voice*]. Pin like a horseshoe.

MRS. MALLET. It's my husband.

MRS. HENDERSON [*in a child's voice*]. He has a message.

MRS. MALLET. Yes.

MRS. HENDERSON [*in a child's voice*]. Lulu cannot hear. He is too far off. He has come near. Lulu can hear now. He says . . . he says, 'Drive that man away!' He is pointing to somebody in the corner, that corner over there. He says it is the bad man who spoilt everything last time. If they won't drive him away, Lulu will scream.

MISS MACKENNA. That horrible spirit again.

ABRAHAM JOHNSON. Last time he monopolised the séance.

MRS. MALLET. He would not let anybody speak but himself.

MRS. HENDERSON [*in a child's voice*]. They have

driven that bad man away. Lulu sees a young lady.

MRS. MALLET. Is not my husband here?

MRS. HENDERSON [*in a child's voice*]. Man with funny pin gone away. Young lady here—Lulu thinks she must be at a fancy dress party, such funny clothes, hair all in curls—all bent down on floor near that old man with glasses.

DR. TRENCH. No, I do not recognise her.

MRS. HENDERSON [*in a child's voice*]. That bad man, that bad old man in the corner, they have let him come back. Lulu is going to scream. O . . . O . . . [*In a man's voice*]. How dare you write to her? How dare you ask if we were married? How dare you question her?

DR. TRENCH. A soul in its agony—it cannot see us or hear us.

MRS. HENDERSON [*upright and rigid, only her lips moving, and still in a man's voice*]. You sit crouching there. Did you not hear what I said? How dared you question her? I found you an ignorant little girl without intellect, without moral ambition. How many times did I not stay away from great men's houses, how many times forsake the Lord Treasurer, how many times neglect the business of the State that we might read Plutarch together!

[*Abraham Johnson half rises. Dr. Trench motions him to remain seated.*

DR. TRENCH. Silence!

ABRAHAM JOHNSON. But, Dr. Trench . . .

DR. TRENCH. Hush—we can do nothing.

MRS. HENDERSON [*speaking as before*]. I taught
you to think in every situation of life not as Hester
Vanhomrigh would think in that situation, but as
Cato or Brutus would, and now you behave like some
common slut with her ear against the keyhole.

JOHN CORBET [*to Miss Mackenna*]. It is Swift,
Jonathan Swift, talking to the woman he called
Vanessa. She was christened Hester Vanhomrigh.

MRS. HENDERSON [*in Vanessa's voice*]. I questioned her, Jonathan, because I love. Why have you
let me spend hours in your company if you did not
want me to love you? [*In Swift's voice*]. When I
rebuilt Rome in your mind it was as though I walked
its streets. [*In Vanessa's voice.*] Was that all, Jonathan? Was I nothing but a painter's canvas? [*In
Swift's voice.*] My God, do you think it was easy? I
was a man of strong passions and I had sworn never
to marry. [*In Vanessa's voice.*] If you and she are
not married, why should we not marry like other
men and women? I loved you from the first moment
when you came to my mother's house and began to
teach me. I thought it would be enough to look at
you, to speak to you, to hear you speak. I followed
you to Ireland five years ago and I can bear it no
longer. It is not enough to look, to speak, to hear.
Jonathan, Jonathan, I am a woman, the women
Brutus and Cato loved were not different. [*In Swift's
voice.*] I have something in my blood that no child
must inherit. I have constant attacks of dizziness; I
pretend they come from a surfeit of fruit when I

was a child. I had them in London. . . . There was a
great doctor there, Dr. Arbuthnot; I told him of
those attacks of dizziness, I told him of worse things.
It was he who explained. There is a line of Dryden's.
. . . [*In Vanessa's voice.*] O, I know—'Great wits
are sure to madness near allied.' If you had children,
Jonathan, my blood would make them healthy. I
will take your hand, I will lay it upon my heart—
upon the Vanhomrigh blood that has been healthy
for generations. [*Mrs. Henderson slowly raises her
left hand.*] That is the first time you have touched
my body, Jonathan. [*Mrs. Henderson stands up and
remains rigid. In Swift's voice.*] What do I care if it
be healthy? What do I care if it could make mine
healthy? Am I to add another to the healthy rascaldom and knavery of the world? [*In Vanessa's voice.*]
Look at me, Jonathan. Your arrogant intellect separates us. Give me both your hands. I will put them
upon my breast. [*Mrs. Henderson raises her right
hand to the level of her left and then raises both to
her breast.*] O, it is white—white as the gambler's
dice—white ivory dice. Think of the uncertainty.
Perhaps a mad child—perhaps a rascal—perhaps a
knave—perhaps not, Jonathan. The dice of the intellect are loaded, but I am the common ivory dice.
[*Her hands are stretched out as though drawing
somebody towards her.*] It is not my hands that draw
you back. My hands are weak, they could not draw
you back if you did not love as I love. You said that
you have strong passions; that is true, Jonathan—no

man in Ireland is so passionate. That is why you need me, that is why you need children, nobody has greater need. You are growing old. An old man without children is very solitary. Even his friends, men as old as he, turn away, they turn towards the young, their children or their children's children. They cannot endure an old man like themselves. [*Mrs. Henderson moves away from the chair, her movements gradually growing convulsive.*] You are not too old for the dice, Jonathan, but a few years if you turn away will make you an old miserable childless man. [*In Swift's voice.*] O God, hear the prayer of Jonathan Swift, that afflicted man, and grant that he may leave to posterity nothing but his intellect that came to him from Heaven. [*In Vanessa's voice.*] Can you face solitude with that mind, Jonathan? [*Mrs. Henderson goes to the door, finds that it is closed.*] Dice, white ivory dice. [*In Swift's voice.*] My God, I am left alone with my enemy. Who locked the door, who locked me in with my enemy? [*Mrs. Henderson beats upon the door, sinks to the floor and then speaks as Lulu.*] Bad old man! Do not let him come back. Bad old man does not know he is dead. Lulu cannot find fathers, mothers, sons that have passed over. Power almost gone. [*Mrs. Mallet leads Mrs. Henderson, who seems very exhausted, back to her chair. She is still asleep. She speaks again as Lulu.*] Another verse of hymn. Everybody sing. Hymn will bring good influence.

[*They sing*]

'If some poor wandering child of Thine
Have spurned to-day the voice divine,
Now, Lord, the gracious work begin;
Let him no more lie down in sin.'

[*During the hymn Mrs. Henderson has been murmuring 'Stella,' but the singing has almost drowned her voice. The singers draw one another's attention to the fact that she is speaking. The singing stops.*]

DR. TRENCH. I thought she was speaking.

MRS. MALLET. I saw her lips move.

DR. TRENCH. She would be more comfortable with a cushion, but we might wake her.

MRS. MALLET. Nothing can wake her out of a trance like that until she wakes up herself. [*She brings a cushion, and she and Dr. Trench put Mrs. Henderson into a more comfortable position.*]

MRS. HENDERSON [*in Swift's voice*]. Stella.

MISS MACKENNA [*to John Corbet*]. Did you hear that? She said 'Stella.'

JOHN CORBET. Vanessa has gone, Stella has taken her place.

MISS MACKENNA. Did you notice the change while we were singing? The new influence in the room?

JOHN CORBET. I thought I did, but it must have been fancy.

MRS. MALLET. Hush!

MRS. HENDERSON [*In Swift's voice*]. Have I wronged you, beloved Stella? Are you unhappy? You have no children, you have no lover, you have no husband. A cross and ageing man for friend—nothing but that. But no, do not answer—you have answered already in that poem you wrote for my last birthday. With what scorn you speak of the common lot of women 'with no adornment but a face—

> 'Before the thirtieth year of life
> A maid forlorn or hated wife.'

It is the thought of the great Chrysostom, who wrote in a famous passage that women loved according to the soul, loved as saints can love, keep their beauty longer, have greater happiness than women loved according to the flesh. That thought has comforted me, but it is a terrible thing to be responsible for another's happiness. There are moments when I doubt, when I think Chrysostom may have been wrong. But now I have your poem to drive doubt away. You have addressed me in these noble words:

> 'You taught how I might youth prolong
> By knowing what is right and wrong;
> How from my heart to bring supplies
> Of lustre to my fading eyes;
> How soon a beauteous mind repairs
> The loss of chang'd or falling hairs;
> How wit and virtue from within
> Can spread a smoothness o'er the skin.'

JOHN CORBET. The words upon the window-pane!
MRS. HENDERSON [*in Swift's voice*]. Then, because you understand that I am afraid of solitude,

afraid of outliving my friends—and myself—you comfort me in that last verse—you overpraise my moral nature when you attribute to it a rich mantle, but O how touching those words which describe your love:

> 'Late dying, may you cast a shred
> Of that rich mantle o'er my head;
> To bear with dignity my sorrow,
> One day alone, then die to-morrow.'

Yes, you will close my eyes, Stella. O, you will live long after me, dear Stella, for you are still a young woman, but you will close my eyes. [*Mrs. Henderson sinks back in chair and speaks as Lulu.*] Bad old man gone. Power all used up. Lulu can do no more. Good-bye, friends. [*Mrs. Henderson speaking in her own voice.*] Go away, go away! [*She wakes.*] I saw him a moment ago, has he spoilt the séance again?

MRS. MALLET. Yes, Mrs. Henderson, my husband came, but he was driven away.

DR. TRENCH. Mrs. Henderson is very tired. We must leave her to rest. [*To Mrs. Henderson.*] You did your best and nobody can do more than that. [*He takes out money.*]

MRS. HENDERSON. No. . . . No. . . . I cannot take any money, not after a séance like that.

DR. TRENCH. Of course you must take it, Mrs. Henderson. [*He puts money on table and Mrs. Henderson gives a furtive glance to see how much it is. She does the same as each sitter lays down his or her money.*]

MRS. MALLET. A bad séance is just as exhausting as a good séance, and you must be paid.

MRS. HENDERSON. No. . . . No. . . . Please don't. It is very wrong to take money for such a failure. [*Mrs. Mallet lays down money.*]

CORNELIUS PATTERSON. A jockey is paid whether he wins or not. [*He lays down money.*]

MISS MACKENNA. That spirit rather thrilled me. [*She lays down money.*]

MRS. HENDERSON. If you insist, I must take it.

ABRAHAM JOHNSON. I shall pray for you to-night. I shall ask God to bless and protect your séances. [*He lays down money.*]

> [*All go out except John Corbet and Mrs. Henderson.*

JOHN CORBET. I know you are tired, Mrs. Henderson, but I must speak to you. I have been deeply moved by what I have heard. This is my contribution to prove that I am satisfied, completely satisfied. [*He puts a note on the table.*]

MRS. HENDERSON. A pound note—nobody ever gives me more than ten shillings, and yet the séance was a failure.

JOHN CORBET [*sitting down near Mrs. Henderson*]. When I say I am satisfied I do not mean that I am convinced it was the work of spirits. I prefer to think that you created it all, that you are an accomplished actress and scholar. In my essay for my Cambridge doctorate I examine all the explanations of

Swift's celibacy offered by his biographers and prove that the explanation you selected was the only plausible one. But there is something I must ask you. Swift was the chief representative of the intellect of his epoch, that arrogant intellect free at last from superstition. He foresaw its collapse. He foresaw Democracy, he must have dreaded the future. Did he refuse to beget children because of that dread? Was Swift mad? Or was it the intellect itself that was mad?

MRS. HENDERSON. Who are you talking of, sir?

JOHN CORBET. Swift, of course.

MRS. HENDERSON. Swift? I do not know anybody called Swift.

JOHN CORBET. Jonathan Swift, whose spirit seemed to be present to-night.

MRS. HENDERSON. What? That dirty old man?

JOHN CORBET. He was neither old nor dirty when Stella and Vanessa loved him.

MRS. HENDERSON. I saw him very clearly just as I woke up. His clothes were dirty, his face covered with boils. Some disease had made one of his eyes swell up, it stood out from his face like a hen's egg.

JOHN CORBET. He looked like that in his old age. Stella had been dead a long time. His brain had gone, his friends had deserted him. The man appointed to take care of him beat him to keep him quiet.

MRS. HENDERSON. Now they are old, now they are young. They change all in a moment as their thought changes. It is sometimes a terrible thing to be out of the body, God help us all.

DR. TRENCH [*at doorway*]. Come along, Corbet. Mrs. Henderson is tired out.

JOHN CORBET. Good-bye, Mrs. Henderson. [*He goes out with Dr. Trench. All the sitters except Miss Mackenna, who has returned to her room, pass along the passage on their way to the front door. Mrs. Henderson counts the money, finds her purse, which is in a vase on the mantelpiece, and puts the money in it.*]

MRS. HENDERSON. How tired I am! I'd be the better of a cup of tea. [*She finds the teapot and puts kettle on fire, and then as she crouches down by the hearth suddenly lifts up her hands and counts her fingers, speaking in Swift's voice.*] Five great Ministers that were my friends are gone, ten great Ministers that were my friends are gone. I have not fingers enough to count the great Ministers that were my friends and that are gone. [*She wakes with a start and speaks in her own voice.*] Where did I put that tea-caddy? Ah! there it is. And there should be a cup and saucer. [*She finds the saucer.*] But where's the cup? [*She moves aimlessly about the stage and then, letting the saucer fall and break, speaks in Swift's voice.*] Perish the day on which I was born!

FIGHTING THE WAVES

*First performed at the Abbey Theatre
on 13th August 1929*

PERSONS IN THE PLAY

THREE MUSICIANS
CUCHULAIN
THE GHOST OF CUCHULAIN
EMER
EITHNE INGUBA
THE FIGURE OF CUCHULAIN
THE WOMAN OF THE SIDHE

FIGHTING THE WAVES

INTRODUCTION

I

I WROTE *The Only Jealousy of Emer* for performance in a private house or studio, considering it, for reasons which I have explained, unsuited to a public stage. Then somebody put it on a public stage in Holland and Hildo van Krop made his powerful masks. Because the dramatist who can collaborate with a great sculptor is lucky, I rewrote the play not only to fit it for such a stage but to free it from abstraction and confusion. I have retold the story in prose which I have tried to make very simple, and left imaginative suggestion to dancers, singers, musicians. I have left the words of the opening and closing lyrics unchanged, for sung to modern music in the modern way they suggest strange patterns to the ear without obtruding upon it their difficult, irrelevant words. The masks get much of their power from enclosing the whole head; this makes the head out of proportion to the body, and I found some difference of opinion as to whether this was a disadvantage or not in an art so distant from reality; that it was not a disadvantage in the case of the Woman of the Sidhe all were agreed. She was a strange, noble, unforgettable figure.

I do not say that it is always necessary when one writes for a general audience to make the words of the dialogue so simple and so matter-of-fact; but it is necessary where the appeal is mainly to the eye and to the ear through songs and music. *Fighting the Waves* is in itself nothing, a mere occasion for sculptor and dancer, for the exciting dramatic music of George Antheil.

II

'It is that famous man Cuchulain. . . .' In the eighties of the last century Standish O'Grady, his mind full of Homer, retold the story of Cuchulain that he might bring back an heroic ideal. His work, which founded modern Irish literature, was hasty and ill-constructed, his style marred by imitation of Carlyle; twenty years later Lady Gregory translated the whole body of Irish heroic legend into the dialect of the cottages in those great books *Cuchulain of Muirthemne* and *Gods and Fighting Men,* her eye too upon life. In later years she often quoted the saying of Aristotle: 'To think like a wise man, but express oneself like the common people,' and always her wise man was heroic man. Synge wrote his *Deirdre of the Sorrows* in peasant dialect, but died before he had put the final touches to anything but the last act, the most poignant and noble in Irish drama. I wrote in blank verse, which I tried to bring as close to common speech as the subject permitted, a number of connected plays—*Deirdre, At the Hawk's Well, The Green Helmet, On Baile's Strand, The Only Jealousy of Emer.* I would have attempted the Battle of the Ford and the Death of Cuchulain, had not the mood of Ireland changed.

III

When Parnell was dragged down, his shattered party gave itself up to nine years' vituperation, and Irish imagination fled the sordid scene. A. E.'s *Homeward Songs by the Way;* Padraic Colum's little songs of peasant life; my own early poems; Lady Gregory's comedies, where, though the dramatic tension is always sufficient, the worst people are no wickeder than children; Synge's *Well of the Saints* and *Playboy of the Western World,* where the worst people are the best company, were as typical of that · time as Lady Gregory's translations. Repelled by what had seemed the sole reality, we had turned to romantic dreaming, to the nobility of tradition.

About 1909 the first of the satirists appeared, 'The Cork Realists,' we called them, men that had come to maturity amidst spite and bitterness. Instead of turning their backs upon the actual Ireland of their day, they attacked everything that had made it possible, and in Ireland and among the Irish in England made more friends than enemies by their attacks. James

Joyce, the son of a small Parnellite organiser, had begun to write, but remained unpublished.

An age is the reversal of an age;
When strangers murdered Emmet, Fitzgerald, Tone,
We lived like men that watch a painted stage.
What matter for the scene, the scene once gone!
It had not touched our lives; but popular rage,
Hysterica passio, dragged this quarry down.
None shared our guilt; nor did we play a part
Upon a painted stage when we devoured his heart.

But even if there had been no such cause of bitterness, of self-contempt, we could not, considering that every man everywhere is more of his time than of his nation, have long kept the attention of our small public, no, not with the whole support, and that we never had, of the Garrets and Cellars. Only a change in European thought could have made that possible. When Stendhal described a masterpiece as a 'mirror dawdling down a lane' he expressed the mechanical philosophy of the French eighteenth century. Gradually literature conformed to his ideal; Balzac became old-fashioned; romanticism grew theatrical in its strain to hold the public; till, by the end of the nineteenth century, the principal characters in the most famous books were the passive analysts of events, or had been brutalised into the likeness of mechanical objects. But Europe is changing its philosophy. Some four years ago the Russian Government silenced the mechanists because social dialectic is impossible if matter is trundled about by some limited force. Certain typical books—*Ulysses,* Mrs. Virginia Woolf's *Waves,* Mr. Ezra Pound's *Draft of XXX Cantos*— suggest a philosophy like that of the *Samkara* school of ancient India, mental and physical objects alike material, a deluge of experience breaking over us and within us, melting limits whether of line or tint; man no hard bright mirror dawdling by the dry sticks of a hedge, but a swimmer, or rather the waves themselves. In this new literature announced with much else by Balzac in *Le Chef-d'œuvre inconnu,* as in that which it superseded, man in himself is nothing.

IV

I once heard Sir William Crookes tell half a dozen people that he had seen a flower carried in broad daylight slowly across the room by what seemed an invisible hand. His chemical research led to the discovery of radiant matter, but the science that shapes opinion has ignored his other research that seems to those who study it the slow preparation for the greatest, perhaps the most dangerous, revolution in thought Europe has seen since the Renaissance, a revolution that may, perhaps, establish the scientific complement of certain philosophies that in all ancient countries sustained heroic art. We may meet again, not the old simple celebration of life tuned to the highest pitch, neither Homer nor the Greek dramatists, something more deliberate than that, more systematised, more external, more self-conscious, as must be at a second coming, Plato's Republic, not the Siege of Troy.

I shall remind the Garrets and Cellars of certain signs, that they may, as a Chinese philosopher has advised, shape things at their beginning, when it is easy, not at the end, when it is difficult. I first name Mr. Sacheverell Sitwell's lovely 'Pastoral'; point out that he has celebrated those Minoan shepherds, those tamers of the wild bulls, their waists enclosed from childhood in wide belts of bronze, that they might attain wasp-like elegance; that he prefers them to the natural easy Sicilian shepherds, preferring as it were cowboys to those that 'watched their flocks by night'; then Dr. Gogarty's praise of 'the Submarine Men trained through a lifetime'; and remind them of their own satisfaction in that praise. Then they might, after considering the demand of the black, brown, green, and blue shirts, 'Power to the most disciplined,' ask themselves whether D'Annunzio and his terrible drill at Fiume may not prove as symbolic as Shelley, whose art and life became so completely identified with romantic contemplation that young men in their late teens, when I was at that age, identified him with poetry itself.

Here in Ireland we have come to think of self-sacrifice, when worthy of public honour, as the act of some man at the moment when he is least himself, most completely the crowd. The heroic act, as it descends through tradition, is an act done because a man is himself, because, being himself, he can ask

nothing of other men but room amid remembered
tragedies; a sacrifice of himself to himself, almost,
so little may he bargain, of the moment to the moment. I think of some Elizabethan play where, when
mutineers threaten to hang the ship's captain, he re-
plies: 'What has that to do with me?' So lonely is
that ancient act, so great the pathos of its joy, that
I have never been able to read without tears a passage in *Sigurd the Volsung* describing how the new-
born child lay in the bed and looked 'straight on the
sun'; how the serving-women washed him, bore him
back to his mother, wife of the dead Sigmund; how
'they shrank in their rejoicing before the eyes of the
child'; 'the best sprung from the best'; how though
'the spring morn smiled . . . the hour seemed awful
to them.'

> But Hiordis looked on the Volsung,
> > on her grief and her fond desire.
> And the hope of her heart was quickened,
> > and her heart was a living fire;
> And she said: 'Now one of the earthly
> > on the eyes of my child hath gazed
> Nor shrank before their glory,
> > nor stayed her love amazed:
> I behold thee as Sigmund beholdeth,—
> > and I was the home of thine heart—
> Woe's me for the day when thou wert not,
> > and the hour when we shall part!'

How could one fail to be moved in the presence
of the central mystery of the faith of poets, painters,
and athletes? I am carried forty years back and hear

a famous old athlete wind up a speech to country lads
—'The holy people have above them the communion
of saints; we the communion of the *Tuatha de
Danaan* of Erin.'

Science has driven out the legends, stories, super-
stitions that protected the immature and the ignorant
with symbol, and now that the flower has crossed our
rooms, science must take their place and demonstrate
as philosophy has in all ages, that States are justified,
not by multiplying or, as it would seem, comforting
those that are inherently miserable, but because
sustained by those for whom the hour seems 'awful,'
and by those born out of themselves, the best born
of the best.

Since my twentieth year, these thoughts have been
in my mind, and now that I am old I sing them to
the Garrets and the Cellars:

> Move upon Newton's town,
> The town of Hobbes and of Locke,
> Pine, spruce, come down
> Cliff, ravine, rock:
> What can disturb the corn?
> What makes it shudder and bend?
> The rose brings her thorn,
> The Absolute walks behind.

v

Yet it may be that our science, our modern philosophy, keep a subconscious knowledge that their
raft, roped together at the end of the seventeenth

century, must, if they so much as glance at that slow-moving flower, part and abandon us to the storm, or it may be, as Professor Richet suggests at the end of his long survey of psychical research from the first experiments of Sir William Crookes to the present moment, that all it can do is, after a steady scrutiny, to prove the poverty of the human intellect, that we are lost amid alien intellects, near but incomprehensible, more incomprehensible than the most distant stars. We may, whether it scrutinise or not, lacking its convenient happy explanations, plunge as Rome did in the fourth century according to some philosopher of that day into 'a fabulous, formless darkness.'

> Should H. G. Wells afflict you
> Put whitewash in a pail;
> Paint: 'Science—opium of the suburbs'
> On some waste wall.

VI

'First I must cover up his face, I must hide him from the sea.' I am deeply grateful for a mask with the silver glitter of a fish, for a dance with an eddy like that of water, for music that suggested, not the vagueness, but the rhythm of the sea. A Dublin journalist showed his scorn for 'the new paganism' by writing: 'Mr. Yeats' play is not really original, for something of the kind doubtless existed in Ancient Babylon,' but a German psycho-analyst has traced the 'mother complex' back to our mother the sea—after all Babylon was a modern inland city—to the loneliness of the first crab or crayfish that climbed ashore and turned lizard; while Gemistus Plethon not only substituted the sea for Adam and Eve, but, according to a friend learned in the Renaissance, made it symbolise the garden's ground or first original, 'that concrete universal which all philosophy is seeking.'

VII

'Everything he loves must fly,' everything he desires; Emer too must renounce desire, but there is another love, that which is like the man-at-arms in the Anglo-Saxon poem, 'doom eager.' Young, we discover an opposite through our love; old, we discover our love through some opposite neither hate nor despair can destroy, because it is another self, a self that we have fled in vain.

*The Music to this play will be
found at the end of the volume*

FIGHTING THE WAVES

PROLOGUE

*Musicians and speaker off stage. There is a curtain
with a wave pattern. A man wearing the Cuchulain
mask enters from one side with sword and shield. He
dances a dance which represents a man fighting the
waves. The waves may be represented by other
dancers: in his frenzy he supposes the waves to be
his enemies: gradually he sinks down as if overcome,
then fixes his eyes with a cataleptic stare upon some
imaginary distant object. The stage becomes dark,
and when the light returns it is empty. The Musicians enter. Two stand one on either side of the curtain, singing.*

FIRST MUSICIAN

A woman's beauty is like a white
Frail bird, like a white sea-bird alone
At daybreak after stormy night
Between two furrows upon the ploughed land:
A sudden storm and it was thrown
Between dark furrows upon the ploughed land.
How many centuries spent
The sedentary soul
In toil of measurement
Beyond eagle or mole,

Beyond hearing or seeing,
Or Archimedes' guess,
To raise into being
That loveliness?

A strange, unserviceable thing,
A fragile, exquisite, pale shell,
That the vast troubled waters bring
To the loud sands before day has broken.
The storm arose and suddenly fell
Amid the dark before day had broken.
What death? What discipline?
What bonds no man could unbind,
Being imagined within
The labyrinth of the mind,
What pursuing or fleeing,
What wounds, what bloody press
Dragged into being
This loveliness?

[*When the curtain is drawn the Musicians
take their place against the wall. One sees
a bed with curtains: the man lying on the
bed is Cuchulain; the part is taken, however, by a different actor, who has a mask
similar to that of the dancer—the Cuchulain mask. Emer stands beside the bed. The
Ghost of Cuchulain crouches near the foot
of the bed.*]

FIRST MUSICIAN [*speaking*]. I call before your
eyes some poor fisherman's house dark with smoke,
nets hanging from the rafters, here and there an oar
perhaps, and in the midst upon a bed a man dead or

swooning. It is that famous man Cuchulain, the best man with every sort of weapon, the best man to gain the love of a woman; his wife Queen Emer is at his side; there is no one with her, for she has sent everyone away, but yonder at the door someone stands and hesitates, wishes to come into the room and is afraid to do so; it is young Eithne Inguba, Cuchulain's mistress. Beyond her, through the open door, the stormy sea. Beyond the foot of the bed, dressed in graveclothes, the ghost of Cuchulain is kneeling.

FIRST MUSICIAN [*singing*]

White shell, white wing!
I will not choose for my friend
A frail, unserviceable thing
That drifts and dreams, and but knows
That waters are without end
And that wind blows.

EMER. Come hither, come sit beside the bed; do not be afraid, it was I that sent for you.

EITHNE INGUBA. No, madam, I have wronged you too deeply to sit there.

EMER. We two alone of all the people in the world have the right to watch together here, because we have loved him best.

EITHNE INGUBA [*coming nearer*]. Is he dead?

EMER. The fishermen think him dead, it was they that put the grave-clothes upon him.

EITHNE INGUBA [*feeling the body*]. He is cold. There is no breath upon his lips.

EMER. Those who win the terrible friendship of the gods sometimes lie a long time as if dead.

EITHNE INGUBA. I have heard of such things; the very heart stops and yet they live after. What happened?

EMER. He fought and killed an unknown man, and found after that it was his own son that he had killed.

EITHNE INGUBA. A son of yours and his?

EMER. So that is your first thought! His son and mine. [*She laughs.*] Did you think that he belonged to you and me alone? He loved women before he heard our names, and he will love women after he has forgotten us both. The man he killed was the son of some woman he loved long ago, and I think he loved her better than he has loved you or me.

EITHNE INGUBA. That is natural, he must have been young in those days and loved as you and I love.

EMER. I think he loved her as no man ever loved, for when he heard the name of the man he had killed, and the name of that man's mother, he went out of his senses utterly. He ran into the sea, and with shield before him and sword in hand he fought the deathless sea. Of all the many men who had stood there to look at the fight not one dared stop him or even call his name; they stood in a kind of stupor, collected together in a bunch like cattle in a storm, until, fixing his eyes as it seemed upon some new enemy, he waded out further still and the waves swept over him.

EITHNE INGUBA. He is dead indeed, and he has been drowned in the sea.

EMER. He is not dead.

EITHNE INGUBA. He is dead, and you have not kissed his lips nor laid your head upon his breast.

EMER. That is some changeling they have put there, some image of somebody or something bewitched in his likeness, a sea-washed log, it may be, or some old spirit. I would throw it into the fire, but I dare not. They have Cuchulain for a hostage.

EITHNE INGUBA. I have heard of such changelings.

EMER. Before you came I called his name again and again. I told him that Queen Maeve and all her Connacht men are marching north and east, and that there is none but he to make a stand against them, but he would not hear me. I am but his wife, and a man grows tired of a wife. But if you call upon him with that sweet voice, that voice that is so dear to him, he cannot help but listen.

EITHNE INGUBA. I am but his newest love, and in the end he will turn to the woman who has loved him longest, who has kept the house for him no matter where he strayed or to whom.

EMER. I have indeed that hope, the hope that some day he and I will sit together at the fire as when we were first married.

EITHNE INGUBA. Women like me awake a violent love for a while, and when the time is over are flung into some corner like an old eggshell. Cuchulain, listen!

EMER. No, not yet; for first I must cover up his face, I must hide him from the sea. I must throw new logs upon the fire and stir the half-burnt logs into a flame. The sea is full of enchantment, whatever lies on that bed is from the sea, but all enchantments dread the hearth-fire.

> [*She pulls the curtains of the bed so as to hide the sick man's face, that the actor may change his mask unseen. She goes to one side of the stage and moves her hand as though putting logs on a fire and stirring it into a blaze. While she makes these movements the Musicians play, marking the movements with drum and flute perhaps. Having finished she stands beside the imaginary fire at a distance from Cuchulain and Eithne Inguba.*

Call on Cuchulain now.

EITHNE INGUBA. Can you hear my voice, Cuchulain?

EMER. Bend over whatever thing lies there, call out dear secrets and speak to it as though it were his very self.

EITHNE INGUBA. Cuchulain, listen!

EMER. Those are timid words. To be afraid because his wife is standing by when there is so great need but proves that he chose badly. Remember who you are and who he is, that we are two women struggling with the sea.

EITHNE INGUBA. O my beloved! Pardon me, pardon me that I could be ashamed when you were in such need. Never did I send a message, never did I call your name, scarce had I a longing for your company but that you have known and come. Remember that never up to this hour have you been silent when I would have you speak, remember that I have always made you talkative. If you are not lying there, if that is some stranger or someone or something bewitched into your likeness, drive it away, remember that for someone to take your likeness from you is a great insult. If you are lying there, stretch out your arms and speak, open your mouth and speak. [*She turns to Emer.*] He does not hear me, no sound reaches him, or it reaches him and he cannot speak.

EMER. Then kiss that image; these things are a great mystery, and maybe his mouth will feel the pressure of your mouth upon that image. Is it not so that we approach the gods?

EITHNE INGUBA [*starting back*]. I felt it was some evil, devilish thing!

EMER. No, his body stirs, the pressure of your mouth has called him. He has thrown the changeling out.

EITHNE INGUBA [*going further off*]. Look at that hand! That hand is withered to the bone.

EMER [*going up to the bed*]. What are you, what do you come for, and from where?

FIGURE OF CUCHULAIN. I am one of the spirits from the sea.

EMER. What spirit from the sea dares lie upon Cuchulain's bed and take his image?

FIGURE OF CUCHULAIN. I am called Bricriu, I am the maker of discord.

EMER. Come for what purpose?

[*Exit Eithne Inguba.*

FIGURE OF CUCHULAIN. I show my face and everything he loves must fly.

EMER. I have not fled your face.

FIGURE OF CUCHULAIN. You are not loved.

EMER. And therefore have no dread to meet your eyes and to demand my husband.

FIGURE OF CUCHULAIN. He is here, your lamentations and that woman's lamentations have brought him in a sort of dream, but you can never win him without my help. Come to my left hand and I will touch your eyes and give you sight.

EMER [*seeing the Ghost of Cuchulain*]. Husband! Husband!

FIGURE OF CUCHULAIN. He seems near, and yet is as much out of reach as though there were a world between. I have made him visible to you. I cannot make you visible to him.

EMER. Cuchulain! Cuchulain!

FIGURE OF CUCHULAIN. Be silent, woman! He can neither see nor hear. But I can give him to you at a price. [*Clashing of cymbals, etc.*] Listen to that. Listen to the horses of the sea trampling! Fand, daughter of Manannan, has come. She is reining in her chariot, that is why the horses trample so. She is come to take Cuchulain from you, to take him away for ever, but I am her enemy, and I can show you how to thwart her.

EMER. Fand, daughter of Manannan!

FIGURE OF CUCHULAIN. While he is still here you can keep him if you pay the price. Once back in Manannan's house he is lost to you for ever. Those who love the daughters of the sea do not grow weary, nor do the daughters of the sea release their lovers.

EMER. There is no price I will not pay.

FIGURE OF CUCHULAIN. You spoke but now of a hope that some day his love may return to you, that some day you may sit by the fire as when first married.

EMER. That is the one hope I have, the one thing that keeps me alive.

FIGURE OF CUCHULAIN. Renounce it, and he shall live again.

EMER. Never, never!

FIGURE OF CUCHULAIN. What else have you to offer?

EMER. Why should the gods demand such a sacrifice?

FIGURE OF CUCHULAIN. The gods must serve those who living become like the dead.

EMER. I will get him in despite of all the gods, but I will not renounce his love.

> [*Fand, the Woman of the Sidhe, enters. Emer draws a dagger and moves as if to strike her.*

FIGURE OF CUCHULAIN [*laughing*]. You think to wound her with a knife! She has an airy body, an invulnerable body. Remember that though your lamentations have dragged him hither, once he has left this shore, once he has passed the bitter sea, once he lands in Manannan's house, he will be as the gods who remember nothing.

> [*The Woman of the Sidhe, Fand, moves round the crouching Ghost of Cuchulain at front of stage in a dance that grows gradually quicker as he awakes. At moments she may drop her hair upon his head, but she does not kiss him. She is accompanied by string and flute and drum. Her mask and clothes must suggest gold or bronze or brass and silver, so that she seems more an idol than a human being. This suggestion may be repeated in her movements. Her hair, too, must keep the metallic suggestion. The object of the dance is that having awakened Cuchulain he will follow Fand out; probably he will seek a kiss and the kiss will be withheld.*

FIGURE OF CUCHULAIN. Cry out that you renounce his love, cry that you renounce his love for ever.

> [*Fand and Cuchulain go out.*

EMER. No, no, never will I give that cry.

FIGURE OF CUCHULAIN. Fool, fool! I am Fand's enemy. I come to tell you how to thwart her and you do nothing. There is yet time. Listen to the horses of the chariot, they are trampling the shore. They are wild and trampling. She has mounted into her chariot. Cuchulain is not yet beside her. Will you leave him to such as she? Renounce his love, and all her power over him comes to an end.

EMER. I renounce Cuchulain's love. I renounce it for ever.

> [*Figure of Cuchulain falls back upon the bed, drawing or partly drawing its curtain that he may change his mask.*
> *Eithne Inguba enters.*

EITHNE INGUBA. Cuchulain, Cuchulain! Remember our last meeting. We lay all night among the sand-hills; dawn came; we heard the crying of the birds upon the shore. Come to me, beloved. [*The curtain of the bed moves.*] Look, look! He has come back, he is there in the bed, he has his own rightful form again. It is I who have won him. It is my love that has brought him back to life!

> [*The figure in the bed pulls back the curtain.*
> *He wears the mask of Cuchulain.*

EMER. Cuchulain wakes!

CUCHULAIN. Your arms, your arms! O Eithne Inguba, I have been in some strange place and am afraid.

EPILOGUE

> [*The Musicians, singing as follows, draw the wave-curtain until it masks the bed, Cuchulain, Eithne Inguba, and Emer.*

FIRST MUSICIAN

Why does your heart beat thus?
Plain to be understood,
I have met in a man's house
A statue of solitude,
Moving there and walking,
Its strange heart beating fast
For all our talking;
O still that heart at last.

O bitter reward
Of many a tragic tomb!
And we though astonished are dumb
And give but a sigh and a word,
A passing word.

Although the door be shut
And all seem well enough,
Although wide world hold not
A man but will give you his love
The moment he has looked at you,
He that has loved the best
May turn from a statue
His too human breast.

O bitter reward
Of many a tragic tomb!
And we though astonished are dumb
And give but a sigh and a word,
A passing word.

What makes your heart so beat?
Is there no man at your side?
When beauty is complete
Your own thought will have died

And danger not be diminished;
Dimmed at three-quarter light,
When moon's round is finished
The stars are out of sight.

O bitter reward
Of many a tragic tomb!
And we though astonished are dumb
And give but a sigh and a word,
A passing word.

[*The Musicians return to their places, Fand,
the Woman of the Sidhe, enters and dances
a dance which expresses her despair for the
loss of Cuchulain. As before there may be
other dancers who represent the waves. It
is called, in order to balance the first dance,
'Fand mourns among the waves.' It is es-
sentially a dance which symbolises, like
water in the fortune-telling books, bitterness. As she takes her final pose of despair
the Curtain falls.*

THE RESURRECTION

*First performed at the Abbey Theatre
on 30th July 1934*

PERSONS IN THE PLAY

Three Musicians
The Hebrew
The Greek
The Syrian
Christ

THE RESURRECTION

I

THIS play, or the first sketch of it, more dialogue than play, was intended for my drawing-room, where my *Hawk's Well* had just been played.

For years I have been preoccupied with a certain myth that was itself a reply to a myth. I do not mean a fiction, but one of those statements our nature is compelled to make and employ as a truth though there cannot be sufficient evidence. When I was a boy everybody talked about progress, and rebellion against my elders took the form of aversion to that myth. I took satisfaction in certain public disasters, felt a sort of ecstasy at the contemplation of ruin, and then I came upon the story of Oisin in Tir-nan-oge and reshaped it into my *Wanderings of Oisin*. He rides across the sea with a spirit, he passes phantoms, a boy following a girl, a hound chasing a hare, emblematical of eternal pursuit, he comes to an island of choral dancing, leaves that after many years, passes the phantoms once again, comes to an island of endless battle for an object never achieved, leaves that after many years, passes the phantoms

once again, comes to an island of sleep, leaves that
and comes to Ireland, to S. Patrick and old age. I
did not pick these images because of any theory, but
because I found them impressive, yet all the while
abstractions haunted me. I remember rejecting, because it spoilt the simplicity, an elaborate metaphor of
a breaking wave intended to prove that all life rose
and fell as in my poem. How hard it was to refrain
from pointing out that Oisin after old age, its il-
lumination half accepted, half rejected, would pass
in death over another sea to another island. Presently
Oisin and his islands faded and the sort of images
that come into *Rosa Alchemica* and *The Adoration
of the Magi* took their place. Our civilisation was
about to reverse itself, or some new civilisation about
to be born from all that our age had rejected, from
all that my stories symbolised as a harlot, and take
after its mother; because we had worshipped a single
god it would worship many or receive from Joachim
de Flora's Holy Spirit a multitudinous influx. A
passage in *La Peau de chagrin* may have started me,
but because I knew no ally but Balzac, I kept silent
about all I could not get into fantastic romance. So
did the abstract ideas persecute me that *On Baile's
Strand,* founded upon a dream, was only finished
when, after a struggle of two years, I had made the
Fool and Blind Man, Cuchulain and Conchubar
whose shadows they are, all image, and now I can
no longer remember what they meant except that
they meant in some sense those combatants who turn

the wheel of life. Had I begun *On Baile's Strand* or not when I began to imagine, as always at my left side just out of the range of the sight, a brazen winged beast [1] that I associated with laughing, ecstatic destruction? Then I wrote, spurred by an external necessity, *Where There is Nothing,* a crude play with some dramatic force, since changed with Lady Gregory's help into *The Unicorn from the Stars.* A neighbourhood inflamed with drink, a country house burnt down, a spiritual anarchy preached! Then after some years came the thought that a man always tried to become his opposite, to become what he would abhor if he did not desire it, and I wasted some three summers and some part of each winter before I had banished the ghost and turned what I had meant for tragedy into a farce: *The Player Queen.* Then unexpectedly and under circumstances described in *A Packet to Ezra Pound* came a symbolical system displaying the conflict in all its forms:

> Where got I that truth?
> Out of a medium's mouth,
> Out of nothing it came,
> Out of the forest loam,
> Out of dark night where lay
> The crowns of Nineveh.

II

> And then did all the Muses sing
> Of Magnus Annus at the spring.

[1] Afterwards described in my poem 'The Second Coming.'

In 1894 Gorky and Lunacharsky tried to correct the philosophy of Marxian socialism by the best German philosophy of their time, founding schools at Capri and Bologna for the purpose, but Lenin founded a rival school at Paris and brought Marxian socialism back to orthodoxy: 'we remain materialist, anything else would lead to religion.' Four or five years later Pius X saw a Commission of Catholic scholars considering the text of the Bible and its attribution to certain authors and dissolved the Commission: 'Moses and the Four Evangelists wrote the Books that are called by their names; any other conclusion would lead to scepticism.' In this way did two great men [1] prepare two great movements, purified of modernism, for a crisis when, in the words of Archbishop Downey, they must dispute the mastery of the world.

So far I have the sympathy of the Garrets and Cellars, for they are, I am told, without exception Catholic, Communist, or both! Yet there is a third myth or philosophy that has made an equal stir in the world. Ptolemy thought the precession of the equinoxes moved at the rate of a degree every hundred years, and that somewhere about the time of Christ and Caesar the equinoctial sun had returned to its original place in the constellations, completing

[1] It is not true, according to Prince Mirsky, that Marxian socialism denies the existence of great men. 'Great men are the embodiment of great social movements, and it is natural that the greater the movement the greater the "great man" produced by it.'

and recommencing the thirty-six thousand years, or three hundred and sixty incarnations of a hundred years apiece, of Plato's man of Ur. Hitherto almost every philosopher had some different measure for the Greatest Year, but this Platonic Year, as it was called, soon displaced all others; it was a Christian heresy in the twelfth century, and in the East, multiplied by twelve as if it were but a month of a still greater year, it became the Manvantra [1] of 432,000 years, until animated by the Indian jungle it generated new noughts and multiplied itself into Kalpas.

It was perhaps obvious, when Plotinus substituted the archetypes of individual men in all their possible incarnations for a limited number of Platonic Ideas, that a Greatest Year for whale and gudgeon alike must exhaust the multiplication table. Whatever its length, it divided, and so did every unit whose multiple it was, into waxing and waning, day and night, or summer and winter. There was everywhere a conflict like that of my play between two principles or 'elemental forms of the mind,' each 'living the other's life, dying the other's death.' I have a Chinese painting of three old sages sitting together, one with a deer at his side, one with a scroll open at the symbol of yen and yin, those two forms that whirl perpetually, creating and re-creating all things. But because of our modern discovery that the equinox shifts

[1] This explanation of the Manvantra comes from an Arab who visited India at the beginning of the tenth century. He is quoted in Pierre Duhem, *Système du Monde,* vol. i. pp. 67 and 68.

its ground more rapidly than Ptolemy believed, one
must, somebody says, invent a new symbolic scheme.
No, a thousand times no; I insist that the equinox
does shift a degree in a hundred years; anything else
would lead to confusion.

All ancient nations believed in the re-birth of the
soul and had probably empirical evidence like that
Lafcadio Hearn found among the Japanese. In our
time Schopenhauer believed it, and McTaggart thinks
Hegel did, though lack of interest in the individual
soul had kept him silent. It is the foundation of
McTaggart's own philosophical system. Cardinal
Mercier saw no evidence for it, but did not think it
heretical; and its rejection compelled the sincere and
noble Von Hügel to say that children dead too young
to have earned Heaven suffered no wrong, never
having heard of a better place than Limbo. Even
though we think temporal existence illusionary it
cannot be capricious; it is what Plotinus called the
characteristic act of the soul and must reflect the
soul's coherence. All our thought seems to lead by
antithesis to some new affirmation of the supernatural. In a few years perhaps we may have much empirical evidence, the only evidence that moves the
mass of men to-day, that man has lived many times;
there is some not yet perfectly examined—I think of
that Professor's daughter in Palermo. This belief
held by Plato and Plotinus, and supported by weighty
argument, resembles the mathematical doctrines of

Einstein before the experimental proof of the curvature of light.

We may come to think that nothing exists but a stream of souls, that all knowledge is biography, and with Plotinus that every soul is unique; that these souls, these eternal archetypes, combine into greater units as days and nights into months, months into years, and at last into the final unit that differs in nothing from that which they were at the beginning: everywhere that antinomy of the One and the Many that Plato thought in his *Parmenides* insoluble, though Blake thought it soluble 'at the bottom of the graves.' Such belief may arise from Communism by antithesis, declaring at last even to the common ear that all things have value according to the clarity of their expression of themselves, and not as functions of changing economic conditions or as a preparation for some Utopia. There is perhaps no final happy state except in so far as men may gradually grow better; escape may be for individuals alone who know how to exhaust their possible lives, to set, as it were, the hands of the clock racing. Perhaps we shall learn to accept even innumerable lives with happy humility—'I have been always an insect in the roots of the grass'—and putting aside calculating scruples be ever ready to wager all upon the dice.

Even our best histories treat men as function. Why must I think the victorious cause the better? Why should Mommsen think the less of Cicero be-

cause Caesar beat him? I am satisfied, the Platonic
Year in my head, to find but drama. I prefer that the
defeated cause should be more vividly described than
that which has the advertisement of victory. No
battle has been finally won or lost; 'to Garret or Cellar a wheel I send.'

III

'What if there is always something that lies outside knowledge, outside order? . . . What if the irrational return? What if the circle begin again?' Years
ago I read Sir William Crookes' *Studies in Psychical
Research*. After excluding every possibility of fraud,
he touched a materialised form and found the heart
beating. I felt, though my intellect rejected what I
read, the terror of the supernatural described by Job.
Just before the war a much respected man of science
entering a room in his own house found there two
girl visitors—I have questioned all three—one lying
asleep on the table, the other sitting on the end of
the table screaming, the table floating in the air, and
'immediately vomited.' I took from the beating heart,
from my momentary terror, from the shock of a man
of science, the central situation of my play: the
young man touching the heart of the phantom and
screaming. It has seemed to me of late that the sense
of spiritual reality comes whether to the individual
or to crowds from some violent shock, and that idea
has the support of tradition.

THE RESURRECTION

Before I had finished this play I saw that its subject-matter might make it unsuited for the public stage in England or in Ireland. I had begun it with an ordinary stage scene in the mind's eye, curtained walls, a window and door at back, a curtained door at left. I now changed the stage directions and wrote songs for the unfolding and folding of the curtain that it might be played in a studio or a drawing-room like my dance plays, or at the Peacock Theatre before a specially chosen audience. If it is played at the Peacock Theatre the Musicians may sing the opening and closing songs, as they pull apart or pull together the proscenium curtain; the whole stage may be hung with curtains with an opening at the left. While the play is in progress the Musicians will sit towards the right of the audience; if at the Peacock, on the step which separates the stage from the audience, or one on either side of the proscenium.

Song for the Unfolding and Folding of the Curtain.

I

I saw a staring virgin stand
Where holy Dionysus died,
And tear the heart out of his side,
And lay the heart upon her hand
And bear that beating heart away;
And then did all the Muses sing
Of Magnus Annus at the spring,
As though God's death were but a play.

II

Another Troy must rise and set,
Another lineage feed the crow,
Another Argo's painted prow
Drive to a flashier bauble yet.
The Roman Empire stood appalled:
It dropped the reins of peace and war
When that fierce virgin and her Star
Out of the fabulous darkness called.

[*The Hebrew is discovered alone upon the
stage; he has a sword or spear. The Musicians make faint drum-taps, or sound a rattle; the Greek enters through the audience
from the left.*

THE HEBREW. Did you find out what the noise
was?

THE GREEK. Yes, I asked a Rabbi.

THE HEBREW. Were you not afraid?

THE GREEK. How could he know that I am called a Christian? I wore the cap I brought from Alexandria. He said the followers of Dionysus were parading the streets with rattles and drums; that such a thing had never happened in this city before; that the Roman authorities were afraid to interfere. The followers of Dionysus have been out among the fields tearing a goat to pieces and drinking its blood, and are now wandering through the streets like a pack of wolves. The mob was so terrified of their frenzy that it left them alone, or, as seemed more likely, so busy hunting Christians it had time for nothing else. I turned to go, but he called me back and asked where I lived. When I said outside the gates, he asked if it was true that the dead had broken out of the cemeteries.

THE HEBREW. We can keep the mob off for some minutes, long enough for the Eleven to escape over the roofs. I shall defend the narrow stair between this and the street until I am killed, then you will take my place. Why is not the Syrian here?

THE GREEK. I met him at the door and sent him on a message; he will be back before long.

THE HEBREW. The three of us will be few enough for the work in hand.

THE GREEK [*glancing towards the opening at the left*]. What are they doing now?

THE HEBREW. While you were down below, James brought a loaf out of a bag, and Nathaniel found a skin of wine. They put them on the table. It was a long time since they had eaten anything. Then they began to speak in low voices, and John spoke of the last time they had eaten in that room.

THE GREEK. They were thirteen then.

THE HEBREW. He said that Jesus divided bread and wine amongst them. When John had spoken they sat still, nobody eating or drinking. If you stand here you will see them. That is Peter close to the window. He has been quite motionless for a long time, his head upon his breast.

THE GREEK. Is it true that when the soldier asked him if he were a follower of Jesus he denied it?

THE HEBREW. Yes, it is true. James told me. Peter told the others what he had done. But when the moment came they were all afraid. I must not blame. I might have been no braver. What are we all but dogs who have lost their master?

THE GREEK. Yet you and I if the mob come will die rather than let it up that stair.

THE HEBREW. Ah! That is different. I am going to draw that curtain; they must not hear what I am going to say. [*He draws curtain.*]

THE GREEK. I know what is in your mind.

THE HEBREW. They are afraid because they do not know what to think. When Jesus was taken they could no longer believe him the Messiah. We can find consolation, but for the Eleven it was always complete light or complete darkness.

THE GREEK. Because they are so much older.

THE HEBREW. No, no. You have only to look into

their faces to see they were intended to be saints. They are unfitted for anything else. What makes you laugh?

THE GREEK. Something I can see through the window. There, where I am pointing. There, at the end of the street. [*They stand together looking out over the heads of the audience.*]

THE HEBREW. I cannot see anything.

THE GREEK. The hill.

THE HEBREW. That is Calvary.

THE GREEK. And the three crosses on the top of it. [*He laughs again.*]

THE HEBREW. Be quiet. You do not know what you are doing. You have gone out of your mind. You are laughing at Calvary.

THE GREEK. No, no. I am laughing because they thought they were nailing the hands of a living man upon the Cross, and all the time there was nothing there but a phantom.

THE HEBREW. I saw him buried.

THE GREEK. We Greeks understand these things. No god has ever been buried; no god has ever suffered. Christ only seemed to be born, only seemed to eat, seemed to sleep, seemed to walk, seemed to die. I did not mean to tell you until I had proof.

THE HEBREW. Proof?

THE GREEK. I shall have proof before nightfall.

THE HEBREW. You talk wildly, but a masterless dog can bay the moon.

THE GREEK. No Jew can understand these things.

THE HEBREW. It is you who do not understand. It is I and those men in there perhaps who begin to understand at last. He was nothing more than a man, the best man who ever lived. Nobody before him had so pitied human misery. He preached the coming of the Messiah because he thought the Messiah would take it all upon himself. Then some day when he was very tired, after a long journey perhaps, he thought that he himself was the Messiah. He thought it because of all destinies it seemed the most terrible.

THE GREEK. How could a man think himself the Messiah?

THE HEBREW. It was always foretold that he would be born of a woman.

THE GREEK. To say that a god can be born of a woman, carried in her womb, fed upon her breast, washed as children are washed, is the most terrible blasphemy.

THE HEBREW. If the Messiah were not born of a woman he could not take away the sins of man. Every sin starts a stream of suffering, but the Messiah takes it all away.

THE GREEK. Every man's sins are his property. Nobody else has a right to them.

THE HEBREW. The Messiah is able to exhaust human suffering as though it were all gathered together in the spot of a burning-glass.

THE GREEK. That makes me shudder. The utmost possible suffering as an object of worship! You are morbid because your nation has no statues.

THE HEBREW. What I have described is what I thought until three days ago.

THE GREEK. I say that there is nothing in the tomb.

THE HEBREW. I saw him carried up the mountain and the tomb shut upon him.

THE GREEK. I have sent the Syrian to the tomb to prove that there is nothing there.

THE HEBREW. You knew the danger we were all in and yet you weakened our guard?

THE GREEK. I have risked the apostles' lives and our own. What I have sent the Syrian to find out is more important.

THE HEBREW. None of us is in our right mind to-day. I have got something in my own head that shocks me.

THE GREEK. Something you do not want to speak about?

THE HEBREW. I am glad that he was not the Messiah; we might all have been deceived to our lives' end, or learnt the truth too late. One had to sacrifice everything that the divine suffering might, as it were, descend into one's mind and soul and make them pure. [*A sound of rattles and drums at first in short bursts that come between sentences, but gradually growing continuous.*] One had to give up all worldly knowledge, all ambition, do nothing of one's own will. Only the divine could have any reality. God had to take complete possession. It must be a terrible thing when one is old, and the tomb round the corner, to think of all the ambitions one has put aside; to think, perhaps, a great deal about women. I want to marry and have children.

THE GREEK [*who is standing facing the audience, and looking out over their heads*]. It is the worshippers of Dionysus. They are under the window now. There is a group of women who carry upon their shoulders a bier with an image of the dead god upon it. No, they are not women. They are men dressed as women. I have seen something like it in Alexandria. They are all silent, as if something were going to happen. My God! What a spectacle! In Alexandria a few men paint their lips vermilion. They imitate women that they may obtain in worship a woman's self-abandonment. No great harm comes of it—but here! Come and look for yourself.

THE HEBREW. I will not look at such madmen.

THE GREEK. Though the music has stopped, some men are still dancing, and some of the dancers have gashed themselves with knives, imagining themselves, I suppose, at once the god and the Titans that murdered him. A little further off a man and woman are coupling in the middle of the street. She thinks the surrender to some man the dance threw into her arms may bring her god back to life. All are from the foreign quarter to judge by face and costume, and are the most ignorant and excitable class of Asiatic Greeks, the dregs of the population. Such people suffer terribly and seek forgetfulness in monstrous ceremonies. Ah, that is what they were waiting for.

The crowd has parted to make way for a singer. It is a girl. No, not a girl; a boy from the theatre. I know him. He acts girls' parts. He is dressed as a girl, but his finger-nails are gilded and his wig is made of gilded cords. He looks like a statue out of some temple. I remember something of the kind in Alexandria. Three days after the full moon, a full moon in March, they sing the death of the god and pray for his resurrection.

[*One of the Musicians sings the following song*]

> Astrea's holy child!
> A rattle in the wood
> Where a Titan strode!
> His rattle drew the child
> Into that solitude.

Barrum, barrum, barrum. [*Drum-taps accompany and follow the words.*]

> We wandering women,
> Wives for all that come,
> Tried to draw him home;
> And every wandering woman
> Beat upon a drum.

Barrum, barrum, barrum. [*Drum-taps as before.*]

> But the murderous Titans
> Where the woods grow dim
> Stood and waited him.
> The great hands of those Titans
> Tore limb from limb.

Barrum, barrum, barrum. [*Drum-taps as before.*]

> On virgin Astrea
> That can succour all
> Wandering women call;
> Call out to Astrea
> That the moon stood at the full.

Barrum, barrum, barrum. [*Drum-taps as before.*]

THE GREEK. I cannot think all that self-surrender and self-abasement is Greek, despite the Greek name of its god. When the goddess came to Achilles in the battle she did not interfere with his soul, she took him by his yellow hair. Lucretius thinks that the gods appear in the visions of the day and night but are indifferent to human fate; that, however, is the exaggeration of a Roman rhetorician. They can be discovered by contemplation, in their faces a high keen joy like the cry of a bat, and the man who lives heroically gives them the only earthly body that they covet. He, as it were, copies their gestures and their acts. What seems their indifference is but their eternal possession of themselves. Man, too, remains separate. He does not surrender his soul. He keeps his privacy.

> [*Drum-taps to represent knocking at the door.*

THE HEBREW. There is someone at the door, but I dare not open with that crowd in the street.

THE GREEK. You need not be afraid. The crowd has begun to move away. [*The Hebrew goes down into the audience towards the left.*] I deduce from our great philosophers that a god can overwhelm man with disaster, take health and wealth away, but man keeps his privacy. If that is the Syrian he may bring such confirmation that mankind will never forget his words.

THE HEBREW [*from amongst the audience*]. It is the Syrian. There is something wrong. He is ill or drunk. [*He helps the Syrian on to the stage.*]

THE SYRIAN. I am like a drunken man. I can hardly stand upon my feet. Something incredible has happened. I have run all the way.

THE HEBREW. Well?

THE SYRIAN. I must tell the Eleven at once. Are they still in there? Everybody must be told.

THE HEBREW. What is it? Get your breath and speak.

THE SYRIAN. I was on my way to the tomb. I met the Galilean women, Mary the mother of Jesus, Mary the mother of James, and the other women. The younger women were pale with excitement and began to speak all together. I did not know what they were saying; but Mary the mother of James said that they had been to the tomb at daybreak and found that it was empty.

THE GREEK. Ah!

THE HEBREW. The tomb cannot be empty. I will not believe it.

THE SYRIAN. At the door stood a man all shining, and cried out that Christ had arisen. [*Faint drumtaps and the faint sound of a rattle.*] As they came down the mountain a man stood suddenly at their side; that man was Christ himself. They stooped down and kissed his feet. Now stand out of my way that I may tell Peter and James and John.

THE HEBREW [*standing before the curtained entrance of the inner room*]. I will not stand out of the way.

THE SYRIAN. Did you hear what I said? Our master has arisen.

THE HEBREW. I will not have the Eleven disturbed for the dreams of women.

THE GREEK. The women were not dreaming. They told you the truth, and yet this man is in the right. He is in charge here. We must all be convinced before we speak to the Eleven.

THE SYRIAN. The Eleven will be able to judge better than we.

THE GREEK. Though we are so much younger we know more of the world than they do.

THE HEBREW. If you told your story they would no more believe it than I do, but Peter's misery would be increased. I know him longer than you do and I know what would happen. Peter would remember that the women did not flinch; that not one amongst them denied her master; that the dream proved their love and faith. Then he would remember that he had lacked both, and imagine that John was looking at him. He would turn away and bury his head in his hands.

THE GREEK. I said that we must all be convinced,

but there is another reason why you must not tell them anything. Somebody else is coming. I am certain that Jesus never had a human body; that he is a phantom and can pass through that wall; that he will so pass; that he will pass through this room; that he himself will speak to the apostles.

THE SYRIAN. He is no phantom. We put a great stone over the mouth of the tomb, and the women say that it has been rolled back.

THE HEBREW. The Romans heard yesterday that some of our people planned to steal the body, and to put abroad a story that Christ had arisen; and so escape the shame of our defeat. They probably stole it in the night.

THE SYRIAN. The Romans put sentries at the tomb. The women found the sentries asleep. Christ had put them asleep that they might not see him move the stone.

THE GREEK. A hand without bones, without sinews, cannot move a stone.

THE SYRIAN. What matter if it contradicts all human knowledge?—another Argo seeks another fleece, another Troy is sacked.

THE GREEK. Why are you laughing?

THE SYRIAN. What is human knowledge?

THE GREEK. The knowledge that keeps the road from here to Persia free from robbers, that has built the beautiful humane cities, that has made the modern world, that stands between us and the barbarian.

THE SYRIAN. But what if there is something it can-

not explain, something more important than anything else?

THE GREEK. You talk as if you wanted the barbarian back.

THE SYRIAN. What if there is always something
that lies outside knowledge, outside order? What if
at the moment when knowledge and order seem complete that something appears? [*He has begun to
laugh.*]

THE HEBREW. Stop laughing.

THE SYRIAN. What if the irrational return? What
if the circle begin again?

THE HEBREW. Stop! He laughed when he saw Calvary through the window, and now you laugh.

THE GREEK. He too has lost control of himself.

THE HEBREW. Stop, I tell you. [*Drums and rattles.*]

THE SYRIAN. But I am not laughing. It is the people out there who are laughing.

THE HEBREW. No, they are shaking rattles and
beating drums.

THE SYRIAN. I thought they were laughing. How
horrible!

THE GREEK [*looking out over heads of audience*].
The worshippers of Dionysus are coming this way
again. They have hidden their image of the dead god,
and have begun their lunatic cry, 'God has arisen!
God has arisen!'

> [*The Musicians who have been saying 'God
> has arisen!' fall silent.*

They will cry 'God has arisen!' through all the streets of the city. They can make their god live and die at their pleasure; but why are they silent? They are dancing silently. They are coming nearer and nearer, dancing all the while, using some kind of ancient step unlike anything I have seen in Alexandria. They are almost under the window now.

THE HEBREW. They have come back to mock us, because their god arises every year, whereas our god is dead for ever.

THE GREEK. How they roll their painted eyes as the dance grows quicker and quicker! They are under the window. Why are they all suddenly motionless? Why are all those unseeing eyes turned upon this house? Is there anything strange about this house?

THE HEBREW. Somebody has come into the room.

THE GREEK. Where?

THE HEBREW. I do not know; but I thought I heard a step.

THE GREEK. I knew that he would come.

THE HEBREW. There is no one here. I shut the door at the foot of the steps.

THE GREEK. The curtain over there is moving.

THE HEBREW. No, it is quite still, and besides there is nothing behind it but a blank wall.

THE GREEK. Look, look!

THE HEBREW. Yes, it has begun to move. [*During what follows he backs in terror towards the left-hand corner of the stage.*]

THE GREEK. There is someone coming through it.

[*The figure of Christ wearing a recognisable but stylistic mask enters through the curtain. The Syrian slowly draws back the curtain that shuts off the inner room where the apostles are. The three young men are towards the left of the stage, the figure of Christ is at the back towards the right.*

THE GREEK. It is the phantom of our master. Why are you afraid? He has been crucified and buried, but only in semblance, and is among us once more. [*The Hebrew kneels.*] There is nothing here but a phantom, it has no flesh and blood. Because I know the truth I am not afraid. Look, I will touch it. It may be hard under my hand like a statue—I have heard of such things—or my hand may pass through it—but there is no flesh and blood. [*He goes slowly up to the figure and passes his hand over its side.*] The heart of a phantom is beating! The heart of a phantom is beating! [*He screams. The figure of Christ crosses the stage and passes into the inner room.*]

THE SYRIAN. He is standing in the midst of them. Some are afraid. He looks at Peter and James and John. He smiles. He has parted the clothes at his side. He shows them his side. There is a great wound there. Thomas has put his hand into the wound. He has put his hand where the heart is.

THE GREEK. O Athens, Alexandria, Rome, something has come to destroy you! The heart of a phantom is beating! Man has begun to die. Your words

are clear at last, O Heraclitus. God and man die each
other's life, live each other's death.

> [*The Musicians rise, one or more singing the
> following words. If the performance is in
> a private room or studio, they unfold and
> fold a curtain as in my dance plays; if at
> the Peacock Theatre, they draw the pro-
> scenium curtain across.*

I

In pity for man's darkening thought
He walked that room and issued thence
In Galilean turbulence;
The Babylonian starlight brought
A fabulous, formless darkness in;
Odour of blood when Christ was slain
Made all Platonic tolerance vain
And vain all Doric discipline.

II

Everything that man esteems
Endures a moment or a day.
Love's pleasure drives his love away,
The painter's brush consumes his dreams;
The herald's cry, the soldier's tread
Exhaust his glory and his might:
Whatever flames upon the night
Man's own resinous heart has fed.

THE CAT AND THE MOON

*First performed at the Abbey Theatre
on 9th May 1926*

TO
JOHN MASEFIELD
who made me a ship

PERSONS IN THE PLAY

THREE MUSICIANS
THE BLIND BEGGAR
THE LAME BEGGAR

THE CAT AND THE MOON

INTRODUCTION

I

THESE plays, which substitute speech and music for painted scenery, should suit Cellars and Garrets, though I do not recommend *The Resurrection* to the more pious Communist or Republican cellars; it may not be as orthodox as I think; I recommend *The Cat and the Moon,* for no audience could discover its dark, mythical secrets. Myth is not, as Vico perhaps thought, a rudimentary form superseded by reflection. Belief is the spring of all action; we assent to the conclusions of reflection but believe what myth presents; belief is love, and the concrete alone is loved; nor is it true that myth has no purpose but to bring round some discovery of a principle or a fact. The saint may touch through myth the utmost reach of human faculty and pass not to reflection but to unity with the source of his being.

The Japanese labour leader and Christian saint Kagawa,[1] perhaps influenced by Vico though his millennium-haunted mind breaks Vico's circle, speaks

[1] 'What is so wonderful about our Saviour,' we writes, 'is that though He lived surrounded by women there was never any scandal.'

of that early phase of every civilisation where a man must follow his father's occupation, where everything is prescribed, as buried under dream and myth. It was because the Irish country people kept something of that early period (had they not lived in Asia until the battle of the Boyne?) that I wrote my *Celtic Twilight,* that Lady Gregory wrote her much richer *Poets and Dreamers,* that she wrote and I annotated those *Visions and Beliefs* in whose collection I had some share. Though Lady Gregory's work is careful and accurate we had little scientific curiosity, but sought wisdom, peace, and a communion with the people. Perhaps a similar emotion made my brother paint country fairs and little streets and the remembered faces of pilots seen at Rosses in his childhood, and Synge create *The Well of the Saints.* I feel at the entrance of the saint in the last act of the play what Lady Gregory must have felt when at the sight of an old man in a wood she said to me, 'That man may have the wisdom of the ages.' Dr. Hyde and his League were different; they sought the peasant, and it is the peasant perhaps who prevails wherever Gaelic is taught, but we sought the peasant's imagination which presses beyond himself as if to the next age. 'Twenty years have I spent upon the battlefields of the world,' said the pensioner in my brother's picture. The choral song, a life lived in common, a futile battle, then thought for its own sake, the last island, Vico's circle and mine, and then the circle joined.

Decline of day,
A leaf drifts down;
O dark leaf clay
On Nineveh's crown!

II

A couple of miles as the crow flies from my Galway house is a blessed well. Some thirty years ago the Gaelic League organised some kind of procession or 'pattern' there, somebody else put a roof over it, somebody else was cured of a lame leg or a blind eye or the falling sickness. There are many offerings at the well-side left by sufferers; I seem to remember bits of cloth torn perhaps from a dress, hairpins, and little pious pictures. The tradition is that centuries ago a blind man and a lame man dreamed that somewhere in Ireland a well would cure them and set out to find it, the lame man on the blind man's back. I wanted to give the Gaelic League, or some like body, a model for little plays, commemorations of known places and events, and wanted some light entertainment to join a couple of dance plays or *The Resurrection* and a dance play, and chose for theme the lame man, the blind man, and the well. It seemed that I could be true to the associations of such places if I kept in mind, while only putting the vaguest suggestion of it into the play, that the blind man was the body, the lame man was the soul. When I had finished I found them in some medieval Irish sermon as a simile of soul and body, and then that they had some like meaning in a Buddhist Sutra. But as the populace might well alter out of all recognition, deprive of all apparent meaning, some philosophical thought or verse, I wrote a little poem where a cat is disturbed by the moon, and in the changing pupils of its eyes seems to repeat the movement of the moon's changes, and allowed myself as I wrote to think of the cat as the normal man and of the moon as the opposite he seeks perpetually, or as having any meaning I have conferred upon the moon elsewhere. Doubtless, too, when the lame man takes the saint upon his back, the normal man has become one with that opposite, but I had to bear in mind that I was among dreams and proverbs, that though I might discover what had been and might be again an abstract idea, no abstract idea must be present. The spectator should come away thinking the meaning as much his own manufacture as that of the blind man and the lame man had seemed mine. Perhaps some early Christian— Bardaisan had speculations about the sun and moon nobody seems to have investigated—thought as I do, saw in the changes of the moon all the cycles: the soul realising its separate being in the full moon, then, as the moon seems to approach the sun and dwindle away, all but realising its absorption in God, only to whirl away once more: the mind of a man, separating itself from the common matrix, through childish imaginations, through struggle—Vico's heroic age—to roundness, completeness, and then externalising, intellectualising, systematising, until at last it lies dead, a spider smothered in its own web:

the choice offered by the sages, either with the soul from the myth to union with the source of all, the breaking of the circle, or from the myth to reflection and the circle renewed for better or worse. For better or worse according to one's life, but never progress as we understand it, never the straight line, always a necessity to break away and destroy, or to sink in and forget.

III

When Lady Gregory's *Visions and Beliefs* had all been collected I began, that I might write my notes, to study spiritualism, of which I had hitherto known nothing. I went from medium to medium, choosing by preference mediums in poor districts where the questioners were small shopkeepers, workmen, and workmen's wives, and found there almost all that Lady Gregory had recorded, though without some of its beauty. It seemed at first that all was taken literally, but I soon found that the medium and some of the questioners knew that something from beyond time was expressing itself in whatever crude symbols they could best understand. I remembered a Sligo visionary who could neither read nor write and said her fairies were big or little according to something in her mind. I began taking notes, piecing together a philosophy resembling that of the villages and of certain passages in the *Spiritual Diary* and *Heaven and Hell* of Swedenborg, and to study natures that seemed upon the edge of the myth-haunted semi-somnambulism of Kagawa's first period. Perhaps now that the abstract intellect has split the mind into categories, the body into cubes, we may be about to turn back towards the unconscious, the whole, the miraculous; according to a Chinese sage darkness begins at midday. Perhaps in my search, as in that first search with Lady Gregory among the cottages, I but showed a first effect of that slight darkening.

IV

'The holy man in the big house,' on page 131, and his friend from Mayo were meant for Edward Martyn and George Moore, both of whom were living when the play was written. I think the audience understood the reference, but when the play is performed where the reference is not understood it might be best to cut out all from 'Do you mind what the beggar told you' down to 'will you answer me that now?' and put into the Blind Beggar's mouth instead the words 'He would soonest.'

THE CAT AND THE MOON

SCENE.—*The scene is any bare place before a wall against which stands a patterned screen, or hangs a patterned curtain suggesting Saint Colman's Well. Three Musicians are sitting close to the wall, with zither, drum, and flute. Their faces are made up to resemble masks.*

FIRST MUSICIAN [*singing*]

The cat went here and there
And the moon spun round like a top,
And the nearest kin of the moon,
The creeping cat, looked up.
Black Minnaloushe stared at the moon,
For wander and wail as he would,
The pure cold light in the sky
Troubled his animal blood.

[*Two beggars enter—a blind man with a lame man on his back. They wear grotesque masks. The Blind Beggar is counting the paces.*

BLIND BEGGAR. One thousand and six, one thousand and seven, one thousand and nine. Look well now, for we should be in sight of the holy well of Saint Colman. The beggar at the cross-roads said it was one thousand paces from where he stood and a few paces over. Look well now, can you see the big ash-tree that's above it?

LAME BEGGAR [*getting down*]. No, not yet.

BLIND BEGGAR. Then we must have taken a wrong turn; flighty you always were, and maybe before the day is over you will have me drowned in Kiltartan River or maybe in the sea itself.

LAME BEGGAR. I have brought you the right way, but you are a lazy man, Blind Man, and you make very short strides.

BLIND BEGGAR. It's great daring you have, and how could I make a long stride and you on my back from the peep o' day?

LAME BEGGAR. And maybe the beggar of the cross-roads was only making it up when he said a thousand paces and a few paces more. You and I, being beggars, know the way of beggars, and maybe he never paced it at all, being a lazy man.

BLIND BEGGAR. Get up. It's too much talk you have.

LAME BEGGAR [*getting up*]. But as I was saying, he being a lazy man—O, O, O, stop pinching the calf of my leg and I'll not say another word till I'm spoken to.

> [*They go round the stage once, moving to drum-taps, and as they move the following song is sung.*

FIRST MUSICIAN [*singing*]

Minnaloushe runs in the grass
Lifting his delicate feet.

Do you dance, Minnaloushe, do you dance?
When two close kindred meet
What better than call a dance?
Maybe the moon may learn,
Tired of that courtly fashion,
A new dance turn.

BLIND BEGGAR. Do you see the big ash-tree?

LAME BEGGAR. I do then, and the wall under it, and the flat stone, and the things upon the stone; and here is a good dry place to kneel in.

BLIND BEGGAR. You may get down so. [*Lame Beggar gets down.*] I begin to have it in my mind that I am a great fool, and it was you who egged me on with your flighty talk.

LAME BEGGAR. How should you be a great fool to ask the saint to give you back your two eyes?

BLIND BEGGAR. There is many gives money to a blind man and would give nothing but a curse to a whole man, and if it was not for one thing—but no matter anyway.

LAME BEGGAR. If I speak out all that's in my mind you won't take a blow at me at all?

BLIND BEGGAR. I will not this time.

LAME BEGGAR. Then I'll tell you why you are not a great fool. When you go out to pick up a chicken, or maybe a stray goose on the road, or a cabbage from a neighbour's garden, I have to go riding on your back; and if I want a goose, or a chicken, or a cabbage, I must have your two legs under me.

BLIND BEGGAR. That's true now, and if we were

whole men and went different ways, there'd be as much again between us.

LAME BEGGAR. And your own goods keep going from you because you are blind.

BLIND BEGGAR. Rogues and thieves ye all are, but there are some I may have my eyes on yet.

LAME BEGGAR. Because there's no one to see a man slipping in at the door, or throwing a leg over the wall of a yard, you are a bitter temptation to many a poor man, and I say it's not right, it's not right at all. There are poor men that because you are blind will be delayed in Purgatory.

BLIND BEGGAR. Though you are a rogue, Lame Man, maybe you are in the right.

LAME BEGGAR. And maybe we'll see the blessed saint this day, for there's an odd one sees him, and maybe that will be a grander thing than having my two legs, though legs are a grand thing.

BLIND BEGGAR. You're getting flighty again, Lame Man; what could be better for you than to have your two legs?

LAME BEGGAR. Do you think now will the saint put an ear on him at all, and we without an Ave or a Paternoster to put before the prayer or after the prayer?

BLIND BEGGAR. Wise though you are and flighty though you are, and you throwing eyes to the right of you and eyes to the left of you, there's many a thing you don't know about the heart of man.

LAME BEGGAR. But it stands to reason that he'd be put out and he maybe with a great liking for the Latin.

BLIND BEGGAR. I have it in mind that the saint will be better pleased at us not knowing a prayer at all, and that we had best say what we want in plain language. What pleasure can he have in all that holy company kneeling at his well on holidays and Sundays, and they as innocent maybe as himself?

LAME BEGGAR. That's a strange thing to say, and do you say it as I or another might say it, or as a blind man?

BLIND BEGGAR. I say it as a blind man, I say it because since I went blind in the tenth year of my age, I have been hearing and remembering the knowledges of the world.

LAME BEGGAR. And you who are a blind man say that a saint, and he living in a pure well of water, would soonest be talking with a sinful man.

BLIND BEGGAR. Do you mind what the beggar told you about the holy man in the big house at Laban?

LAME BEGGAR. Nothing stays in my head, Blind Man.

BLIND BEGGAR. What does he do but go knocking about the roads with an old lecher from the county of Mayo, and he a woman-hater from the day of his birth. And what do they talk of by candle-light and by daylight? The old lecher does be telling over all the sins he committed, or maybe never committed at all, and the man of Laban does be trying to head him off and quiet him down that he may quit telling them.

LAME BEGGAR. Maybe it is converting him he is.

BLIND BEGGAR. If you were a blind man you wouldn't say a foolish thing the like of that. He wouldn't have him different, no, not if he was to get all Ireland. If he was different, what would they find to talk about, will you answer me that now?

LAME BEGGAR. We have great wisdom between us, that's certain.

BLIND BEGGAR. Now the Church says that it is a good thought, and a sweet thought, and a comfortable thought, that every man may have a saint to look after him, and I, being blind, give it out to all the world that the bigger the sinner the better pleased is the saint. I am sure and certain that Saint Colman would not have us two different from what we are.

LAME BEGGAR. I'll not give in to that, for, as I was saying, he has a great liking maybe for the Latin.

BLIND BEGGAR. Is it contradicting me you are? Are you in reach of my arm? [*swinging stick*].

LAME BEGGAR. I'm not, Blind Man, you couldn't touch me at all; but as I was saying—

FIRST MUSICIAN [*speaking*]. Will you be cured or will you be blessed?

LAME BEGGAR. Lord save us, that is the saint's voice and we not on our knees.   [*They kneel.*

BLIND BEGGAR. Is he standing before us, Lame Man?

LAME BEGGAR. I cannot see him at all. It is in the ash-tree he is, or up in the air.

FIRST MUSICIAN. Will you be cured or will you be blessed?

LAME BEGGAR. There he is again.

BLIND BEGGAR. I'll be cured of my blindness.

FIRST MUSICIAN. I am a saint and lonely. Will you become blessed and stay blind and we will be together always?

BLIND BEGGAR. No, no, your Reverence, if I have to choose, I'll have the sight of my two eyes, for those that have their sight are always stealing my things and telling me lies, and some maybe that are near me. So don't take it bad of me, Holy Man, that I ask the sight of my two eyes.

LAME BEGGAR. No one robs him and no one tells him lies; it's all in his head, it is. He's had his tongue on me all day because he thinks I stole a sheep of his.

BLIND BEGGAR. It was the feel of his sheepskin coat put it into my head, but my sheep was black, they say, and he tells me, Holy Man, that his sheepskin is of the most lovely white wool so that it is a joy to be looking at it.

FIRST MUSICIAN. Lame Man, will you be cured or will you be blessed?

LAME BEGGAR. What would it be like to be blessed?

FIRST MUSICIAN. You would be of the kin of the blessed saints and of the martyrs.

LAME BEGGAR. Is it true now that they have a book

and that they write the names of the blessed in that book?

FIRST MUSICIAN. Many a time I have seen the book, and your name would be in it.

LAME BEGGAR. It would be a grand thing to have two legs under me, but I have it in my mind that it would be a grander thing to have my name in that book.

FIRST MUSICIAN. It would be a grander thing.

LAME BEGGAR. I will stay lame, Holy Man, and I will be blessed.

FIRST MUSICIAN. In the name of the Father, the Son, and the Holy Spirit I give this Blind Man sight and I make this Lame Man blessed.

BLIND BEGGAR. I see it all now, the blue sky and the big ash-tree and the well and the flat stone,—all as I have heard the people say—and the things the praying people put on the stone, the beads and the candles and the leaves torn out of prayer-books, and the hairpins and the buttons. It is a great sight and a blessed sight, but I don't see yourself, Holy Man— is it up in the big tree you are?

LAME BEGGAR. Why, there he is in front of you and he laughing out of his wrinkled face.

BLIND BEGGAR. Where, where?

LAME BEGGAR. Why, there, between you and the ash-tree.

BLIND BEGGAR. There's nobody there—you're at your lies again.

LAME BEGGAR. I am blessed, and that is why I can see the holy saint.

BLIND BEGGAR. But if I don't see the saint, there's something else I can see.

LAME BEGGAR. The blue sky and green leaves are a great sight, and a strange sight to one that has been long blind.

BLIND BEGGAR. There is a stranger sight than that, and that is the skin of my own black sheep on your back.

LAME BEGGAR. Haven't I been telling you from the peep o' day that my sheepskin is that white it would dazzle you?

BLIND BEGGAR. Are you so swept with the words that you've never thought that when I had my own two eyes, I'd see what colour was on it?

LAME BEGGAR [*very dejected*]. I never thought of that.

BLIND BEGGAR. Are you that flighty?

LAME BEGGAR. I am that flighty. [*Cheering up.*] But am I not blessed, and it's a sin to speak against the blessed.

BLIND BEGGAR. Well, I'll speak against the blessed, and I'll tell you something more that I'll do. All the while you were telling me how, if I had my two eyes, I could pick up a chicken here and a goose there, while my neighbours were in bed, do you know what I was thinking?

LAME BEGGAR. Some wicked blind man's thought.

BLIND BEGGAR. It was, and it's not gone from me

yet. I was saying to myself I have a long arm and a strong arm and a very weighty arm, and when I get my own two eyes I shall know where to hit.

LAME BEGGAR. Don't lay a hand on me. Forty years we've been knocking about the roads together, and I wouldn't have you bring your soul into mortal peril.

BLIND BEGGAR. I have been saying to myself I shall know where to hit and how to hit and who to hit.

LAME BEGGAR. Do you not know that I am blessed? Would you be as bad as Caesar and as Herod and Nero and the other wicked emperors of antiquity?

BLIND BEGGAR. Where'll I hit him, for the love of God, where'll I hit him?

> [*Blind Beggar beats Lame Beggar. The beating takes the form of a dance and is accompanied on drum and flute. The Blind Beggar goes out.*

LAME BEGGAR. That is a soul lost, Holy Man.

FIRST MUSICIAN. Maybe so.

LAME BEGGAR. I'd better be going, Holy Man, for he'll rouse the whole country against me.

FIRST MUSICIAN. He'll do that.

LAME BEGGAR. And I have it in my mind not to even myself again with the martyrs, and the holy confessors, till I am more used to being blessed.

FIRST MUSICIAN. Bend down your back.

LAME BEGGAR. What for, Holy Man?

FIRST MUSICIAN. That I may get up on it.

LAME BEGGAR. But my lame legs would never bear the weight of you.

FIRST MUSICIAN. I'm up now.

LAME BEGGAR. I don't feel you at all.

FIRST MUSICIAN. I don't weigh more than a grasshopper.

LAME BEGGAR. You do not.

FIRST MUSICIAN. Are you happy?

LAME BEGGAR. I would be if I was right sure I was blessed.

FIRST MUSICIAN. Haven't you got me for a friend?

LAME BEGGAR. I have so.

FIRST MUSICIAN. Then you're blessed.

LAME BEGGAR. Will you see that they put my name in the book?

FIRST MUSICIAN. I will then.

LAME BEGGAR. Let us be going, Holy Man.

FIRST MUSICIAN. But you must bless the road.

LAME BEGGAR. I haven't the right words.

FIRST MUSICIAN. What do you want words for? Bow to what is before you, bow to what is behind you, bow to what is to the left of you, bow to what is to the right of you. [*The Lame Beggar begins to bow.*

FIRST MUSICIAN. That's no good.

LAME BEGGAR. No good, Holy Man?

FIRST MUSICIAN. No good at all. You must dance.

LAME BEGGAR. But how can I dance? Ain't I a lame man?

FIRST MUSICIAN. Aren't you blessed?

LAME BEGGAR. Maybe so.

FIRST MUSICIAN. Aren't you a miracle?

LAME BEGGAR. I am, Holy Man.

FIRST MUSICIAN. Then dance, and that'll be a miracle.

> [*The Lame Beggar begins to dance, at first clumsily, moving about with his stick, then he throws away the stick and dances more and more quickly. Whenever he strikes the ground strongly with his lame foot the cymbals clash. He goes out dancing, after which follows the First Musician's song.*

FIRST MUSICIAN [*singing*]

Minnaloushe creeps through the grass
From moonlit place to place.
The sacred moon overhead
Has taken a new phase.
Does Minnaloushe know that his pupils
Will pass from change to change,
And that from round to crescent,
From crescent to round they range?
Minnaloushe creeps through the grass
Alone, important and wise,
And lifts to the changing moon
His changing eyes.

The bravest from the gods but ask:
A house, a sword, a ship, a mask.

MUSIC TO *FIGHTING THE WAVES*

By George Antheil

FIGHTING THE WAVES

GEORGE ANTHEIL

OVERTURE
Marcato poco adagio (♩=80)

143

Con mosso, tumultuous sea-like (♩=63)

dark   fur - rows

up   on   the   ploughed

land.   Largo (♩=48)

How many-cen-tu-ries   spent   The se-den-ta-ry soul   In   toil of meas-

ure-ment   Beyond ea-gle   or—mole.

147

Be-yond hear-ing or — see-ing, Or Arch-i-medes' guess, To raise in-to

be-ing That love-li-ness?

Più mosso molto (♩.= 88)

A strange, un - ser-vice-a-ble

thing, A fra-gile, ex qui - site,— pale—

shell, ———— That the vast trou-bled wa-ters bring

What bonds no man could un-bind, Be—ing im-a-gined with—in The la-by-rinth of the mind,____ What pur-su-ing or flee——ing, What wounds,

what blood-y press Drag - ged in-to be - ing This love-li-ness?

The Ghost of Cuchulain may perhaps enter here, Emer, Eithne Inguba, and the Figure on the bed being discovered on the stage

A tempo marcato (♩ = 80)

Larghetto espressivo (♩ = 66)

White shell, white wing! ___ I

will not choose ___ for my friend ___ A

151

frail un - ser - vice - a - ble thing_____ That

drifts and dreams, and but knows That wa - ters are

with - out end_____ And that wind blows_____

FAND'S DANCE

"Who remembers nothing"

Largo (♩ = 48-52)

(*massively*)

⊕ Repeat first six
bars again ad lib.

Poco più mosso, espressivo

Why does your heart beat thus? Plain to be under-stood,

155

- though the door be shut____ And all seem well e-

-nough,____ Al-though wide world hold not A

man but will give you his love The mo-ment he has

looked at you, He that has__ loved the best

May turn from a sta-tue His too hu-man breast.___

espressivo poco meno mosso

O bit-ter re-ward Of ma-ny a tra-gic tomb!

a tempo (piu mosso)

What makes your heart so beat?

Più mosso (♩ = 100)

Is there no man at your side?When beau-

ty is com-plete Your own thought will have died And dan-ger
not be dim-in - ished;

A tempo largo

Dimm'd at three-quar-ter light, When moon's round is fin-ished The
stars are out of sight. O bit-ter re-ward!

repeat section Ⓐ to Ⓑ
here, if desired

FAND'S FINAL DANCE
Con mosso (♩=116)

159

dying away

Curtain

Marcato poco adagio

poco rit.

mp poco accel.

f a tempo